A natural history of
Dinosaurs

A natural history of Dinosaurs

Richard Moody
B.Sc Ph.D F.G.S

CHARTWELL
BOOKS INC.

Acknowledgments

The author would like to thank Mr L. Backshall and Mrs S. Pickering for their assistance in the preparation of this manuscript. He is also indebted to the staff of the Palaeontology Department of the British Museum (Natural History), and in particular to Dr A. Charig and Mr C. A. Walker for the provision of important scientific papers and help in the clarification of certain points of detail. Whilst writing this book the author was influenced by the ideas of numerous research workers who deserve praise for their originality and dedication.

Line drawings by Jennifer Middleton (pages 11, 12, 14 bottom, 15 bottom, 16, 17, 18, 20 bottom, 21, 23, 33, 36, 37), Linda Parry (pages 10, 14 top, 15 top, 20 top, 22, 24, 29), and Tony Morris (pages 28, 30, 31, 32, 34).

To Zoé, Rebecca and James

Published by the Hamlyn Publishing Group Limited
London · New York · Sydney · Toronto
Astronaut House, Feltham, Middlesex, England

Published in the United States by
Chartwell Books Inc.,
A Division of Book Sales Inc.,
110 Enterprise Avenue
Secaucus
New Jersey 07094

Copyright ©
The Hamlyn Publishing Group Limited 1977
ISBN 0 600 32935 6
ISBN 0–89009–132–3 (Chartwell edition)
Library of Congress Catalog Card No. 77–78124

Phottypeset by Filmtype Services Limited, Scarborough, England
Printed in Hong Kong

Contents

Introduction

During the last ten years or so, new discoveries, improved preparatory techniques and detailed morphological studies have forced palaeontologists to reconsider many of the accepted theories attributed to the form, function and ecology of dinosaurs. For too long researchers were mentally strait-jacketed by the belief that, like living reptiles, the dinosaurs were cold-blooded animals, with a metabolic rate similar to that of the crocodiles or turtles. This belief tended to overshadow all else, and only in a few cases were dinosaurs thought to be extremely active creatures. The studies of dinosaur bone structure and of dinosaur communities have, however, stimulated much scientific thought and some workers now believe that many, if not all, the dinosaurs were warm-blooded.

Arguments for and against this idea command respect and, although the claim that dinosaurs were endothermic (warm blooded) may be refuted, the stimulus it has given to vertebrate palaeontology is immeasurable.

Dinosaur endothermy has been expressed with some artistic licence in recent years, and animals once interpreted as slow, sluggish creatures now fly through the air with either gay abandon or murderous intent. This artistic treatment may reflect the freedom of thinking of the latter half of this century in much the same way as the models of Waterhouse Hawkins, at Crystal Palace, London, illustrate the beginning of dinosaur palaeontology over a hundred years ago. Recent illustrations not only reflect the departure from previously accepted interpretations, they also reveal the number and importance of new discoveries and the emphasis now placed on functional studies. Some dinosaurs were heavy, cumbersome creatures but others, often small and lightly built, appear to have been capable of sustained activity.

Among the hundreds of species comprising the Dinosauria, food chains existed in which agile meat eaters preyed upon the more heavily built herbivores. Dinosaurs evolved rapidly during the Mesozoic Era to become the dominant element of the terrestrial fauna, with individuals exhibiting spectacular adaptations to their environment or mode of life. These changes in physical appearance were often associated with behavioural functions and community development. The success and survival of a group such as the dinosaurs during 150 million years of geological time is a reflection of their ability to adapt within a changing world.

What is a dinosaur?

Of the various vertebrate animals that live today, the reptiles can be described as cold-blooded creatures that lay an egg protected by an outer shell (the amniote egg). In the geological record the advent of this, the 'reptilian egg', was of great importance in the conquest of the land and gave the reptiles a distinct advantage over the archaic Amphibia. Unlike the spawn of frogs and toads, the reptile egg is protected by a porous shell; it also contains a food supply for the developing embryo. As in the chicken's egg, the food reserve is called the yolk whilst the egg 'white', or albumen, provides water essential to the growth of the young reptile. Thin membranes surround and separate the various layers within the shell and enable the

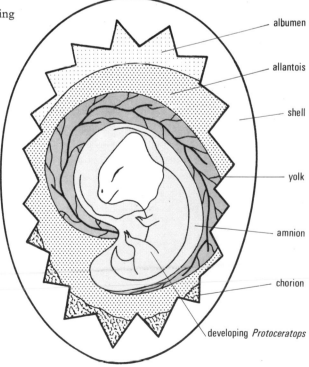

A diagrammatic reconstruction of the developing egg of *Protoceratops*.

albumen

allantois

shell

yolk

amnion

chorion

developing *Protoceratops*

reptile embryo to perform all the functions essential to life.

Being cold-blooded creatures, reptiles lack an internal means of regulating the temperature of the body. Consequently they are dependent on the external climate for maintaining their body temperature, and the rate at which they function varies accordingly. At night or during cold spells reptiles are slow, sluggish creatures, but on warm days they absorb heat to raise their body temperature and speed up the rate at which the body processes are carried out. Even when the body is functioning at an optimum temperature, however, the structure of some reptile hearts prevents sustained periods of activity. 'Impure' blood from the body is constantly mixed with 'cleansed' blood from the lungs and, like humans with a 'hole in the heart', reptiles like the lizards and snakes tire quickly. Even the most advanced living reptiles, the crocodiles, have a small hole which connects the two main blood vessels taking blood to various parts of the body.

Evidence of the amniote egg and the structure of the reptile heart is limited or unknown among fossil discoveries; the determination and classification of extinct forms being based on skeletal characters. Eggs of turtles and of dinosaurs such as *Protoceratops* from Mongolia may provide important information, but in most cases the form and character of the skull and post-cranial skeleton is all-important in the association of the living and fossil vertebrates referred to the class Reptilia. Four types of skulls are known within the class, each representing a line of evolutionary development. Of the four the diapsid type, in which two pairs of skull openings occur, is characteristic of the living crocodiles, lizards and snakes, the fossil pterosaurs (flying reptiles), and the dinosaurs and their ancestors.

Diapsids originated in the Permian Period, and before the end of the Triassic had become the dominant reptile line, a position they have retained until the present day. Within the diapsid lineage the snakes and lizards form one distinct group, with the crocodiles, pterosaurs, dinosaurs and thecodonts forming another. The last four are known as the *archosaurs* and of these the dinosaurs were the most varied and the most successful. They were, to say the least, a very unique group of reptiles.

History of discovery

Long before Richard Owen had identified the dinosaurs as a 'distinct tribe or suborder of Saurian Reptiles' on 2nd August 1841, a number of large bones and footprints, subsequently referred to the group, had been found in Europe and North America. Unfortunately scientific knowledge was somewhat limited, and these dinosaurian bones and traces were attributed to giant men, fishes and lizards – the footprints actually being identified as those of 'Noah's Raven'.

The earliest recorded discovery of dinosaur remains is attributed to the Reverend Dr Robert Plot, who in 1676 described the lower portion of a very large femur. The bone was illustrated by both Plot and Brooks (1763) and both men may have felt justified in their claim that it belonged to a giant man. The legend associated with the figure in Brooks, refers to the bone as '*Scrotum humanum*'. Sadly the bone has been lost but from the illustrations and descriptions that survive, it would appear to be very similar to the thigh bone of the great carnosaur *Megalosaurus*.

After the discovery of '*Scrotum humanum*' by Plot, a century elapsed before the next written references were made to huge bones in various American scientific journals. These references noted the discovery of large bones from sediments of the Triassic and Cretaceous Periods. Many of these specimens have since been lost, but those from the Triassic of the Connecticut Valley have been preserved and subsequently identified as the bones of the dinosaur *Anchisaurus*.

Aquatic reptiles of enormous proportions had been identified during the latter half of the 18th century. The discovery of the great 'Meuse Lizard', *Mosasaurus*, from the Upper Cretaceous rocks of Maastricht, Holland, in 1770 was an important event in the history of vertebrate palaeontology. The enormous jaws of this strange lizard, extracted from the subterranean caverns of St Peter's Mountain, belonged to a creature some 6–8 metres (19·5–26 feet) in length, and were taken as an indication of the exotic character of life before the great flood. In 1784 the discovery of a small, bat-like pterosaur in Jurassic sediments of southern Germany, supported the view that reptiles of the remote past differed markedly from those of the present time.

The beautiful preservation of the 'Meuse Lizard', the German pterosaur and the ichthyosaurs discovered by Mary Anning in Lyme Regis, England, in 1810 enabled early palaeontologists to associate them with living reptiles; whereas the disarticulated, often fragmentary material later identified as belonging to dinosaurs was useless in the light of existing knowledge. Only when Gideon Mantell, a Sussex doctor and keen palaeontologist, insisted that some teeth discovered by his wife were similar to those of the common iguana, did the idea of giant terrestrial reptiles really take hold. Unlike the teeth of the iguana, those discovered by Mrs Mantell in 1822 were very large, and indicated that the creature to which they belonged stood over 10 metres (33 feet) in height. Dr Mantell did not publish the account of his creature, *Iguanodon,* until 1825; further finds enabled him to reconstruct his monster, but unfortunately he mounted the now characteristic thumb bone as a horn on its nose.

Mantell's delay in publication was in part due to lack of agreement among the eminent palaeontologists and naturalists whom he approached for help. Among them was Dr William Buckland, a reader in geology at Oxford University who, in 1824, described the

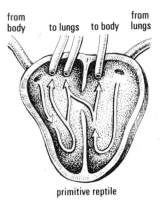

primitive reptile

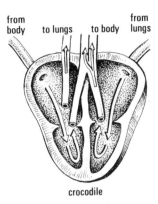

crocodile

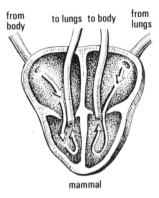

mammal

The primitive reptile heart is not separated into four distinct chambers. The heart of a crocodile is separated into chambers, but a small aperture links the blood vessels that carry blood to the body. In mammals the heart has four clearly separated chambers, and only 'cleansed', well-oxygenated blood is returned to the body. This enables mammals to maintain a higher level of activity.

anapsid skull as found in turtles

synapsid skull as found in
mammal-like reptiles

diapsid skull as found in dinosaurs

euryapsid skull as found
in plesiosaurs

The four basic types of
skulls found in living and
fossil reptiles. They are
recognized by the variation
in the bone pattern behind
the eye, and by the number
of foramina (openings)
present.

gigantic terrestrial saurian *Megalosaurus*. The first megalosaurid bones were extracted from the Stonesfield Slate quarries of Oxfordshire, but others uncovered by Mantell came from the Tilgate Forest in Sussex, a location from which Mantell was to extract many beautiful fossil remains.

With the evidence of *Iguanodon* and *Megalosaurus*, even the most doubting palaeontologists were persuaded that great reptiles once ruled the world. Unfortunately Buckland, in his account of *Megalosaurus*, had failed to emphasise the differences that existed between this ancient beast and the modern lizards. This omission was to delay the recognition of the existence of the fossil record of a distinct and hitherto unknown group.

The discovery of giant bones continued throughout the late 1820's and 1830's, and by 1841 nine distinct genera had been recognized. Of these, *Megalosaurus, Iguanodon* and *Hylaeosaurus* were to be used by Owen in his establishment of the suborder Dinosauria. In a momentous speech, delivered at Plymouth on 2nd August 1841, Owen listed the characters of these peculiar terrestrial reptiles. The name of the suborder is derived from the Greek *deinos* – 'terrible', and *sauros* – 'lizard'. Owen, in his recognition of a new suborder, indicated that the dinosaurs were not lizards but sadly his choice of name, evocative as it is, was to prove unfortunate. For in some ways it failed to separate these bizarre reptiles from the great aquatic saurians such as *Mosasaurus*, and also modern lizards. The Victorians were often guilty of referring to the dinosaurs as gigantic lizards, forgetting completely Owen's belief that they were the crown of reptilian creation.

In 1854 the Crystal Palace, originally built by Joseph Paxton for the Great Exhibition of 1851, was reopened at Sydenham, Kent. Queen Victoria and Prince Albert attended the ceremony and shared with thousands of Londoners the first public viewing of the models of the great prehistoric monsters recreated by Waterhouse Hawkins. The models were constructed under the careful supervision of Owen who, along with the Prince Consort, viewed the reopening as an opportunity to introduce the public to the giants of the past.

During the same year a young American geologist, F. V. Hayden, was sent on an expedition into Montana where, along the banks of a tributary of the Missouri, he discovered numerous teeth which, in 1858, he was to present to the Academy of Natural Sciences, Philadelphia. Joseph Leidy, the director at that time, ascribed the bones to dinosaurs, and so announced to the world that the great reptiles had not been confined to one area during geological time. Leidy's contribution, like that of Owen's, continued for a number of years and included the description of the duck-billed dinosaur *Hadrosaurus foulkei*. He was also to lecture and perhaps influence the young Edward Drinker Cope, who was in turn to become one of the greatest palaeontologists of his age.

Cope is known not only for his scientific work but also for his scientific feuding with a contemporary, Othniel Charles Marsh. The feud was in some ways the result of a character clash between the brilliant, prolific Cope and the deliberate, single-minded Marsh; it was also the inevitable outcome of intense academic competition. Throughout the early stages of their careers, which began at the end of the American Civil War, these accomplished scientists enjoyed a somewhat guarded friendship. This ended in the late 1870's when Marsh and the ageing Leidy criticized a Cope reconstruction. From then on both men resorted to open warfare, using both the existing media and academic connections to score victories over each other. Their hired collectors searched the Great Plains and Rocky Mountains for new localities and each man viewed the other's successes with great jealousy. Great collections, and dozens of important papers, resulted from the competition between the two men, and twenty-eight new genera were described before their deaths. Of these Marsh described nineteen and is, in respect of numbers, to be regarded as the victor although Cope published some 1400 papers on various scientific subjects.

Whilst Leidy and then Cope and Marsh led the way in America, great scientists such as Thomas Henry Huxley and Louis Dollo worked in Europe. Huxley used the dinosaurs such as *Iguanodon* and *Compsognathus* in his defence of Darwin's evolutionary theory, and Dollo described the magnificent iguanodont discovery from Bernissart in Belgium. This rivalled the discoveries by Marsh at Como Bluff, in eastern Wyoming, and by the close of the Bernissart excavation was to yield thirty-one skeletons. The specimens were found in a fissure infill some 300 metres (984 feet) below ground level by coal miners in 1877. Casts of Bernissart iguanodonts are to be found in many museums throughout the world.

In the 1890's and early 1900's new expeditions were to visit the American west and make important discoveries from sites such as 'Bone Cabin' quarry, Wyoming, and Vernal in Utah. The former was discovered by Walter Granger who was searching the area in 1897 on behalf of The American Museum of Natural History in New York. For six years museum groups worked the area, returning with tonnes of dinosaur bones for the museum vaults and exhibition halls.

The Vernal discovery was, if anything, even more spectacular, being found in the summer of 1909 by Earl Douglass who prospected on behalf of the Carnegie Museum in Pittsburgh. As at Bone Cabin, tonnes of bones were removed from the sandstones near Split Mountain. Sauropod dinosaurs are among the most spectacular creatures to have lived on this planet, and the skeletons of *Apatosaurus louisiae* and *Diplodocus carnegeii* from the Vernal site represent two of the finest individuals ever uncovered by Man. Because of the great importance of the quarry at Vernal,

President Woodrow Wilson declared the area surrounding it the Dinosaur National Monument, the actual declaration taking place on 4th October 1915. It remains until today, an unusual gem in the history of American vertebrate palaeontology.

Not all the discoveries made at this time were on the massive scale recorded above, but some were of unique importance to vertebrate palaeontologists. The mummified duck-billed dinosaur found by Charles Sternberg in Kansas in 1908, for example, offered a number of clues on soft part anatomy and mode of preservation. Sternberg also discovered the first of the crested duck-bills in 1913. By 1920 the dinosaur localities of North America and Canada had yielded an incredible array of creatures. These ranged from the diminutive *Ornitholestes*, 3·4 metres (11 feet) long, to the gigantic sauropods such as *Diplodocus*, 30 metres (98 feet) long, and included the plant-eating horned dinosaurs and voracious meat eaters.

The discovery of dinosaurs in North America, England and Belgium should not be viewed in isolation, for during the 19th and the early part of the 20th centuries, dinosaur skeletons were unearthed in Germany, Hungary, Asia, Africa and South America. In Germany one of the earliest dinosaurs, *Plateosaurus*, was described in 1837, whilst in Africa dinosaur bones were discovered in 1854. German expeditions were mounted to various parts of the world, and in 1907 an expedition from the Museum fur Naturkunde in Berlin discovered many superb specimens in the Jurassic sediments of East Africa. Significantly these resembled many of the individuals unearthed by Professor Cope at Como Bluff, Wyoming. In South America numerous skeletons were collected in the Argentine between 1882 and the 1920's. 1922 saw the discovery of dinosaurs and dinosaur eggs in the wastelands of Outer Mongolia, an area from which successive expeditions from America, Russia, China and Poland have collected a wealth of material. A German expedition to western China in the 1940's discovered a relative of the genus *Plateosaurus*. This discovery supported evidence from South Africa that the prosauropod dinosaurs were widely distributed in Upper Triassic times.

The more recent expeditions to Asia bring our story up to date, for the joint Polish-Mongolian expeditions of 1965 and 1971 link the early searches of the 1920's with those of the last two decades. The finds of the last two Gobi searches are now world famous, and include the only record of two dinosaurs locked in mortal combat. Dinosaur discoveries continue to make headlines throughout the world, and monsters of hitherto unknown proportions or unusual character are still being found. In 1964 the agile 'terrible claw', *Deinonychus*, was discovered in the Lower Cretaceous of Montana; whilst *Deinocheirus*, the 'terrible hand', from the Upper Cretaceous of Mongolia, first discovered in 1965, suggests that dinosaurs even more fearsome than *Tyrannosaurus* existed on Earth.

At the present time vertebrate palaeontologists still search for dinosaur remains, they also undertake research on existing collections, and have entered upon a serious debate on the importance of 'mammalian-like' canal systems in dinosaur bones, and the predator-prey numbers within dinosaur communities.

Geological time and the origin of the dinosaurs

Geological time is calculated in millions of years, and the age of the Earth is estimated at 4700 million years. This is subdivided into two *eons* named the Cryptozoic, 'the age of hidden life', and the Phanerozoic or 'age of obvious life'. Most geologists use the term Precambrian when referring to the Cryptozoic and have estimated that this eon lasted 4000 million years. The first signs of life are found in Precambrian sediments, with simple organisms, somewhat similar to blue-green algae, first appearing in rocks 3300 million years old. At approximately 1300 million years many-celled creatures appeared, and from then on the diversification of animal life increased quite dramatically.

The Phanerozoic Eon is subdivided into three *eras*, each of which is characterized by the presence of particular groups of animals and plants. Each era is subdivided into *periods*, and some periods are divided into 'lower' (early), 'middle' and 'upper' (late). The oldest era is the Palaeozoic which, translated, means the 'old life'. It is divided into five periods and lasted approximately 355 million years.

The Mesozoic Era, or 'middle life', is also known as the Age of Reptiles, and spanned 160 million years of geological time and embraced the Triassic, Jurassic and Cretaceous Periods. Sixty five million years ago saw the dawn of the Cainozoic Era, or 'new life'.

Life in the Palaeozoic

At the start of the Palaeozoic Era creatures with hard skeletal parts appeared in great numbers. The form of individual species and the complex structure of the communities to which they belonged suggest that their development started during the Precambrian. Throughout the Lower Palaeozoic, invertebrate animals dominated marine life. Limited evidence from Cambrian and Ordovician sediments heralds the evolution of the first vertebrates in shallow coastal environments. During the Silurian and Devonian Periods the fishes emerged as successful scavengers and predators, with families expanding into the seas and also into various freshwater niches. Towards the end of the Devonian the first amphibian

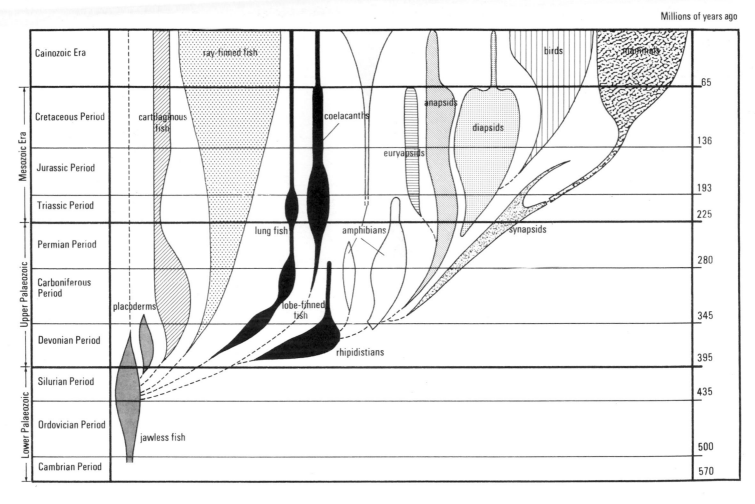

Cainozoic Era	ray-finned fish	birds · mammals
	cartilaginous fish	coelacanths · anapsids
Cretaceous Period		diapsids
Jurassic Period		euryapsids
Triassic Period		
Permian Period	lung fish · amphibians	synapsids
Carboniferous Period	lobe-finned fish	
Devonian Period	placoderms · rhipidistians	
Silurian Period		
Ordovician Period	jawless fish	
Cambrian Period		

Mesozoic Era — Upper Palaeozoic — Lower Palaeozoic

65 · 136 · 193 · 225 · 280 · 345 · 395 · 435 · 500 · 570

Above Vertebrate evolution. The fortunes of each group of vertebrates are reflected in the range and prominence of their respective bands.

appeared, its origin being associated with the migration of the lobe-finned fishes into shallow-water environments. This migration may have been the result of intense competition with the ray-finned fishes, and the need to find an alternative food source. Frequent seasonal droughts may have encouraged the development of limbs which, together with the evolution of lungs, would have enabled these 'new' creatures to leave their dried-up pools and search for new habitats for, like recent frogs and toads, Palaeozoic amphibians needed to keep their skins moist, and to lay their eggs in water.

Suitable environments for the evolution and adaptation of the amphibians to new habitats existed in both the Upper Devonian and Lower Carboniferous. Early amphibians such as *Ichthyostega* spent much of their time in water, but the presence of well-developed

limbs and of an eardrum must be considered as adaptations to a life on land. Aquatic amphibians thrived during the Upper Carboniferous – an age dominated geographically by vast tracts of lush, humid, coal-forming swamps. Immature individuals discovered in sediments formed under these conditions appear to be juvenile stages of terrestrial forms, and suggest that whilst the aquatic species were content to remain in the protection of their watery dens, other amphibians were invading new ecological niches. Fossils of adult terrestrial amphibians have been discovered in Permian deposits, but their appearance is too late for them to be the ancestors of the reptiles, as the first of these creatures appeared at the end of the Lower Carboniferous.

Reptilian remains from Nova Scotia indicate that the split from an amphibian ancestor

Right *Eustenopteron*, a lobe-finned fish from the Devonian Period, possessed lungs and strong fins which enabled it to migrate across short distances of land during drought conditions.

Far right Amphibians such as *Ichthyostega* lived part of their lives on land. Amphibians were the dominant land vertebrates during the late Devonian and Carboniferous Periods.

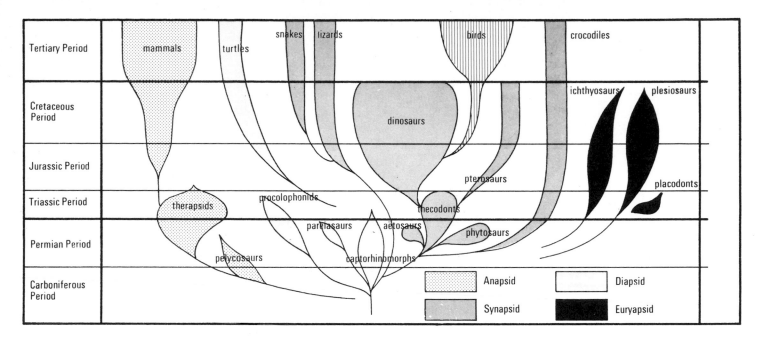

		mammals	turtles	snakes	lizards	birds	crocodiles	
Tertiary Period								
Cretaceous Period					dinosaurs		ichthyosaurs plesiosaurs	
Jurassic Period						pterosaurs	placodonts	
Triassic Period		therapsids	procolophonids		thecodonts			
Permian Period			pareiasaurs	aetosaurs	phytosaurs			
		pelycosaurs		captorhinomorphs				
Carboniferous Period						Anapsid — Diapsid		
						Synapsid — Euryapsid		

Above Evolution of the reptiles. The range and prominence of each band reflect the fortunes of the group concerned.

took place early in the history of the parent group, for by the end of the Lower Carboniferous, reptiles of the anapsid and synapsid type had already evolved. The first reptiles were rather small creatures, and forms such as *Hylonomus* are thought to have lived most of their lives in ponds and lakes. *Hylonomus* fed on insects and laid its eggs on land. Unlike the eggs of its amphibian ancestor, those of *Hylonomus* were protected by an outer shell.

The spread of the reptiles into terrestrial niches was a gradual event related to their ability to catch food and survive the rigours of climatic change. The fossil record is incomplete, but it is probable that numerous experimental or intermediate animals evolved before the appearance of a truly terrestrial reptile. In environmental terms, the swamplands of the Upper Carboniferous afforded the evolving reptiles ideal conditions from which they could first probe, and then exploit more arid regions. The 'missing link' animals between the amphibians and *Hylonomus* laid their eggs on land in order to protect them from egg-feeders, whilst the descendants of the first reptile developed the capacities to withstand desiccation and overcome problems related to the fertilization of eggs on land.

During the Late Carboniferous both anapsid lines and synapsid lines of the Reptilia diversified. Flesh-eating and herbivorous reptiles ap-

peared in both groups during the Lower Permian, with *Limnocelis*, an anapsid, being representative of the first carnivores. It was probably a semi-aquatic creature with crocodilian habits, feeding mainly on fairly large, fish-eating amphibians. Synapsid carnivores such as *Ophiacodon* and *Dimetrodon* evolved slightly later in time. *Ophiacodon* contested the same niche as *Limnocelis* and probably replaced the primitive anapsid. *Dimetrodon*, however, was a truly terrestrial creature growing to over 3 metres (10 feet) in length. It possessed a large, sail-like structure on its back which was used to regulate body temperature. *Dimetrodon* was the dominant carnivore of the time and could be regarded as the last link in a complex food chain. Herbivorous reptiles also appeared in the Lower Permian; some were anapsids, others synapsids. *Cotylorhynchus* and *Edaphosaurus* represent two groups of primitive synapsids. *Cotylorhynchus* grew to almost 3 metres (10 feet) in length and weighed an estimated 317 kilogrammes (700 pounds). It was a rather primitive creature, and like *Limnocelis*, was replaced by the more active edaphosaurs. *Edaphosaurus* was a sail-back reptile like *Dimetrodon*, but unlike its flesh-eating cousin it was clearly semi-aquatic. The teeth of both sail-backs were rather specialized and clearly related to their feeding habits. Those of *Edaphosaurus* were used to crush

Far left *Hylonomus* was one of the first reptiles; its remains have been found in the remnants of tree trunks preserved in sediments approximately 300 million years old.

Left In the early Permian, *Dimetrodon* was the ruling carnivore. The sail on its back helped in the control of body temperature.

plant material and the shells of freshwater mussels and snails; batteries of similar sized teeth lined the powerful jaws. In *Dimetrodon* the teeth were differentiated into incisors, canines and cheek teeth. The canines were used in the kill, the incisors to bite through the flesh and the cheek teeth to grind the food into smaller pieces. The changes in the character of the dentition in many pelycosaurs indicate that they are distant relatives of the mammals. During the Permian the evolution within the synapsid line was quite rapid and, by the middle of the period, the pelycosaurs had been succeeded by more advanced stocks.

Middle Permian faunas from North America, Russia and South Africa reveal the extent to which the assemblages had changed. Advanced synapsids were common to all three areas, but the large herbivorous anapsids – the pareiasaurs – appear to be restricted to Russia and South Africa. In North America the various fossil assemblages suggest the presence of two lowland faunas, one aquatic, the other terrestrial. The same story may be true of Russia, but in South Africa the community had a terrestrial base.

Like *Cotylorhynchus* and *Edaphosaurus* of the Early Permian, the anapsids were rather bulky creatures. Their size was a reflection of the need for herbivores to consume much more food than carnivores, and of the time needed to digest plant material inside the body. Of the advanced synapsids, both herbivorous and flesh-eating individuals occur in Middle Permian. *Moschops* was a typical plant eater; again it is a rather bulky creature and its peg-like teeth indicate that it fed on soft vegetation. It was a large animal and probably spent its life in lowland regions around ponds and lakes. In Russia the remains of *Moschops* are associated with those of fishes, amphibians and large synapsid carnivores called titanosuchids. The latter also thrived in South Africa and it is most likely that they fed on pareiasaurs and synapsids related to *Moschops*. *Titanosuchus* was a 'sprawler', pulling its large body along in lizard-like fashion. Like *Moschops*, it was an advanced synapsid (or therapsid) reptile and exhibited a number of new advances along the road to the mammals. The therapsids did not have the characteristic sail of the pelycosaurs and it would be safe to say that they developed another method of controlling their body temperature. Later, more agile therapsids

such as *Lycaenops* from the Upper Permian were possibly warm-blooded. *Lycaenops* did not sprawl on the ground like *Titanosuchus*, for its limbs were drawn closer to the body and the trunk lifted well above the ground. Forms such as *Lycaenops* succeeded *Titanosuchus* and its relatives as the dominant predator during the Upper Permian, in the same way as dicynodont therapsids replaced the pareiasaurs as the prominent group of herbivores.

Anapsid reptiles were of limited importance during the Triassic Period. the pareiasaurs and the descendants of *Hylonomus* had vanished; the line being represented by insect-eating forms such as *Hypsognathus*. Triassic reptile communities were at first dominated by the advanced therapsids. Herds of dicynodonts still roamed over the South African landscape but now their main danger came, not from *Lycaenops*, but from the truly mammal-like reptiles called the cynodonts and bauriomorphs.

In the main these animals ate meat, but some lived as scavengers, feeding from any available food source. Both groups developed a false or secondary palate between the air passages and the mouth – a feature which enabled them to breathe and chew at the same time. The muscles of the jaws had also grown larger, and the cynodonts in particular developed teeth with cusps, which enabled them to break their food into smaller pieces. These improvements of the jaw musculature and teeth indicate that the mammal-like reptiles chewed their food over and over again. Most workers now believe that cynodonts such as *Thrinaxodon* and *Cynognathus* were covered in hair. The cynodonts ruled Triassic communities until the close of the Middle Triassic and the expansion of the ancestors of the dinosaurs (the diapsid thecodontians).

The ancestors of the dinosaurs

The thecodontians first appeared in the Late Permian in the form of the primitive *Proterosuchus*. It lived in the lakes and rivers of the Southern Hemisphere and looked rather like a crocodile. *Proterosuchus* fed on fishes and amphibians. On land it was a rather cumbersome creature with a 'sprawling' posture, its legs outspread and its trunk touching the ground. In water *Proterosuchus* was a competent predator, but when it ventured into the lowland domain of the therapsids it would not be able to compete. Some descendants of *Proterosuchus*, such as *Chasmatosaurus*, were also aquatic in habit, but others like *Erythrosuchus* dwelt on land. During the Lower Triassic *Chasmatosaurus* occupied the same niche in many regions of the world. In the Southern Hemisphere it inhabited the same freshwater lakes as the rather hippopotamus-like *Lystrosaurus*. The latter was a dicynodont, and its remains have been found in Africa, India and Antarctica.

Erythrosuchus grew to over 4 metres (13 feet) in length. It was a 'sprawler' but, like *Chasmatosaurus*, still capable of killing the

Cynognathus was the largest cynodont (advanced mammal-like reptile); it was probably covered with hair and was warm-blooded. *Cynognathus* lived during the Lower Triassic, over 200 million years ago.

herbivorous dicynodonts. In South Africa, *Chasmatosaurus* lived at the same time as the advanced form *Euparkeria*, which, unlike its thecodont cousin, ran on two legs. In fact *Euparkeria* is recognized as the first bipedal animal to occur in the fossil record. It is also considered by many to be the immediate ancestor of the Dinosauria. *Euparkeria* was rather small at 1 metre (3 feet) long, and lightly built. Whilst feeding, it moved around on all fours, but when disturbed or challenged it would adopt a two-legged gait. The back legs were larger than the fore limbs and it would have been very difficult for it to run on all fours. The position of the limbs on *Euparkeria* represents a considerable improvement over the 'sprawling' movement of earlier reptiles. It was an important evolutionary step, and by the Middle Triassic four-legged thecodontians had also appeared in which the limbs had been pulled inwards towards the body, and the trunk lifted well clear of the ground. An example of a four-legged thecodont with the 'semi-improved' condition was *Mandasuchus* from the Middle Triassic of South Africa.

The bipedal thecodontians probably became more and more specialized, with the most advanced forms having their limbs drawn under the body. Effectively this would have raised the animal on to its toes and increased the length of its stride. The attainment of the 'semi-improved' and possibly the 'fully improved' condition would have given the thecodontians a great advantage over the mammal-like reptiles. Coupled with possible physiological improvements it must have made the socket-toothed reptiles impossible adversaries. *Lagerpeton* and *Ornithosuchus* from the Middle and Upper Triassic are examples of very fast-running thecodontians. *Ornithosuchus* was larger than *Euparkeria* and had a protective cover of thickened plates over its back. It was a voracious predator, and was instrumental in the demise of the mammal-like reptiles. This faunal replacement took place soon after the start of the Upper Triassic. A few palaeontologists believe that *Ornithosuchus* was the first of the flesh-eating dinosaurs, but others doubt this, claiming that it was a highly specialized thecodontian representing an evolutionary peak within the group.

The evolution of the thecodontians as agile, terrestrial carnivores has been associated with the climatic changes of the Permian and early Triassic. Information retrieved from the study of fossil-rich sediments of the Upper Permian indicates that they were mainly deposited in deltas and along coastal plains. These lowland areas were fertile feeding grounds for the mammal-like reptiles and the first thecodontians. With the onset of the Triassic the picture changed, the stable environments disappeared and in many regions desiccation forced the evolving archosaurs to search for new habitats. Some were able to meet the challenge and soon dominated the mammal-like reptiles in the competition for food and territory.

The dinosaurs appear

The success of the thecodontians was instrumental in the origin of even more advanced archosaurs. For in killing off the existing prey populations during the latter half of the Triassic Period, the thecodontians created food resource problems with too many carnivores chasing too few herbivores. The gradual reduction and final extinction of the dicynodonts and other plant eaters in the second half of the Triassic, prompted various archosaur groups to adopt new modes of life. Some specialized thecodontians, like the phytosaurs and aëtosaurs, returned to the aquatic and semi-aquatic niches of earlier stocks. The phytosaurs looked like crocodiles except that their nostrils were placed between the eyes. They lived in lakes and rivers, and fed on fishes. The aëtosaurs were also of crocodilian appearance but, unlike the phytosaurs, they fed on the soft vegetation to be found in marshland areas. Apart from the phytosaurs and their herbivorous relatives, other groups were forced either to occupy new territories and new niches or suffer constant attack from the successful thecodontians. These groups were the crocodiles, pterosaurs and dinosaurs.

The appearance of various dinosaur stocks in the Middle Triassic suggests that they actually originated at an earlier time. From the fossil material collected from the Middle Triassic, however, it is possible to reconstruct the evolution of both saurischian (lizard-hipped) and ornithischian (bird-hipped) forms. The common ancestor for both groups was undoubtedly a thecodont, with *Euparkeria* or a close relative being selected by many palaeontologists as a likely candidate.

Saurischian dinosaurs are characterized by a hip girdle which is somewhat similar to that of other reptiles. The girdle is fused to the vertebral column, and it acts as an area of muscle attachment and forms a socket for the articulation of the thigh bone. In the saurischians, three bones form the girdle; the ilium, which is fused to the vertebrae, the ischium which is directed posteriorly, and the elongate pubis which is projected downwards and forwards. The structure of the saurischian girdle is different to that of the ornithischians, in which the pelvis is bird-like. The ilium of the 'bird-hipped' dinosaurs is still fused to the vertebral column, and the ischium still directed

sprawling condition

semi-improved condition

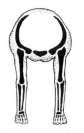

fully improved condition

Above During the evolution of the ruling reptiles (the archosaurs), limb posture and locomotion were to change considerably from the sprawling condition, through the semi-improved condition, to the fully improved condition.

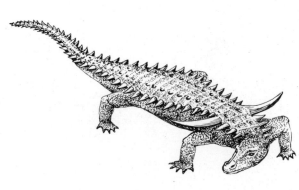

Left Aëtosaurs such as *Desmatosuchus* were a specialized branch of the thecodontians which returned to a semi-aquatic mode of life.

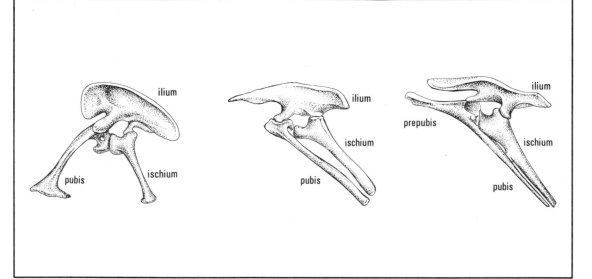

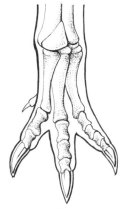

foot of a typical theropod
(e.g. *Tyrannosaurus*)

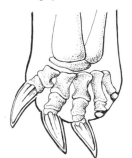

foot of a typical sauropod
(e.g. *Brachiosaurus*)

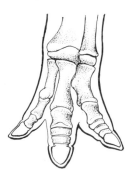

foot of a typical ornithopod
(e.g. *Iguanodon*)

backwards, but the pubis now lies beneath the ischium. In advanced ornithischians the pubis has two prongs, the posterior prong represents the old bone, and the forward prong a new development.

Two types of saurischians are recognized and both have representation in Triassic faunas. The first group, the prosauropod dinosaurs, appeared simultaneously in a number of regions. Initially they possessed teeth similar to those of the thecodontians and they were capable of either a four- or two-legged gait. *Thecodontosaurus* was one of the first saurischians and was probably the first dinosaur to eat plants. It lived in Europe during the Middle Triassic and its intermediate character has earned it and its relatives the title of the prosauropods. By the late Triassic prosauropods were to be found as far afield as Europe, China, South Africa and America. During the millions of years that passed between the Middle and Upper Triassic the prosauropods changed considerably – *Plateosaurus* from Europe and similar forms from South Africa and China having grown to twice or three times the size of their ancestors. In the Jurassic the prosauropods were succeeded by the true sauropods, included in which are the greatest land dwellers of all time with *Brachiosaurus* as the largest of them all.

The second group of saurischians are the theropods or 'beast-footed' dinosaurs. They appeared at the same time as the prosauropods; the first theropods were the small, lightly built coelurosaurs. Like the specialized thecodontians described previously, the coelurosaurs were bipedal meat eaters. The first recorded coelurosaurs were discovered in Upper Triassic sediments of North America. Coelurosaur genera are known throughout the Age of Reptiles, their size and agility being particularly suited to the roles of scavenger, egg stealer and killer of small mammals. Other theropods – the gigantic carnosaurs – are also recorded from the Upper Triassic; their size and sheer physical strength making them the arch-predators of all time. Like their coelurosaur cousins, the carnosaurs prospered

throughout the Age of Reptiles, with numerous genera existing on various continental land masses.

Ornithischians are rare in the Triassic but three genera, *Pisanosaurus*, *Fabrosaurus* and *Heterodontosaurus*, indicate that the group originated around the same time as the first saurischians. Triassic ornithischians were characterized by the length of their hind limbs. Their toes were exceptionally long and indicate that they ran very quickly. All ornithischians were plant eaters and it is likely that the earliest types retained their long limbs as a defence mechanism against the evolving theropods. In the Jurassic many ornithischians were quadrupedal (four-legged) and slow, but they defended themselves by developing various forms of protection including body armour and long horns.

The relationship between the prosauropods, sauropods and theropods has been accepted by most palaeontologists, although the actual link between the saurischians and the ornithischians is subject to much controversy. Some believe that a single dinosaur stock evolved from the thecodontians and that this stock subdivided into the Prosauropoda, Theropoda and Ornithischia; whilst others believe that each group evolved independently from a common thecodontian ancestor. The arguments are centred around the detailed study of the structure of the earliest dinosaurs and their positions in the stratigraphic record. Each new discovery is like a new clue to the solution of a very difficult crossword.

Whatever the true relationships of the earliest dinosaurs are, it is obvious that they became functionally superior to earlier groups of reptiles. By the close of the Triassic they had spread throughout the world, their success being linked perhaps with an improved circulation of the blood, warm-bloodedness, or the care of the nest and young by the female. Their migration was also aided by geographical and climatic factors. Until the end of the Triassic the continents as we know them were joined together, forming the supercontinent Pangea. No oceans existed between areas such as South

America, South Africa and Antarctica, and terrestrial animals were able to migrate freely. Equable, subtropical conditions existed throughout much of the supercontinent and this eased the problems of the migrating thecodontians and dinosaurs.

Throughout the Jurassic and Cretaceous Periods the dinosaurs showed a great capacity to cope with change. For 140 million years they were to rule the world, with hundreds of new species evolving to occupy many different ecological niches. Some, like the sauropods, were to become giants, their very size protecting them from all but the largest of predators. Others were to live in great herds wandering across the Cretaceous landscapes of North America and Asia. Size and numbers were important factors in the success of specific families, but others were characteristically small, filling the roles of scavengers and insectivores. The Age of Dinosaurs is noted for the appearance and replacement of successive faunas. Dinosaurs were important components of Mesozoic terrestrial communities, and we shall look closely at their individual roles and their relationships to other Mesozoic animals.

At the end of the Cretaceous Period the dinosaurs vanished, and the Cainozoic Era witnessed the dramatic radiation of the mammals to fill the empty niches. In recent years palaeontologists have suggested that the birds evolved from dinosaur ancestors. A few believe that the birds represent the final success story in the long history of the Dinosauria.

Dinosaur communities

Biologists define a community as an association of different populations – the term population being applied when significant numbers of a particular animal or plant occur in one or more localities. The populations that are associated within the community live in close contact and can be expected to affect each others' way of life. Each individual animal of the population needs an energy source to survive, and the way in which energy is obtained is critical to the structure of the community. Associations of animals and plants exist all around us and we can see that whilst plants rely on the rays of the sun to produce food, some animals eat plants, and carnivores eat herbivores. Other organisms act as scavengers and decomposers and each one is seen to occupy its own niche.

In the study of a fossil-rich deposit, however, the amount of available data is significantly less. Death is usually followed by the decay or destruction of the animal remains, and only a small percentage of the animals and plants that lived during the last 600 million years has been preserved in the fossil record. Sometimes the fossils of these organisms are found in abundance, and palaeontologists can attempt the reconstruction of the community.

Apart from the fossils a great deal of information is derived from a study of the rock type in which they are preserved.

Accumulations of dinosaur bones and related animals and plants have been found throughout the Age of Dinosaurs. Careful collecting, together with the recording of important field data, has enabled researchers to identify the links that existed between the dinosaurs and the environment in which they lived. Dinosaur communities, like animal communities of today, varied in relation to terrain and vegetation. They also changed with time, new groups replacing those which failed to meet with change or which could not compete with the new species. The associations described below are based on the evidence recorded in the fossil record. Not all fossils are abundant or complete, but such is the skill of the experts that even a single tooth may be sufficient for identification. The discovery of a solitary bone or of an individual skeleton is not evidence of a community, but it may be useful in plotting geographic distributions and possible migration routes.

Triassic dinosaurs

In the account of the origin and radiation of the early reptiles, we saw that the first dinosaurs shared their environment with the thecodontians, mammal-like reptiles and amphibians. At first the number of dinosaur species was limited, but because of the links that existed between land masses they were able to spread throughout much of the world. The continents enjoyed a uniform climate with most areas experiencing rather arid conditions. During short, wet seasons great rivers crossed the dry terrain and their banks were covered with lush vegetation. At the mouths of the rivers vast flood plains occurred, and deltas extended seawards. Beyond the river banks and deltas, the countryside was rather barren with a cover of hardy vegetation. In some areas shallow lakes formed at the foot of large mountain ranges.

The vegetation of the second half of the Triassic consisted mostly of spore-bearing plants such as the ferns, club mosses and horsetails. Primitive seed plants also occurred with the cycads, early gingkoes and conifers spreading into the countryside beyond the river banks. As with the vertebrates, the floras of this time provide evidence of climatic stability throughout much of the world.

The first dinosaurs of the Middle Triassic were discovered in South America and southern Africa. In southern Africa the reptile communities included herbivores such as the dicynodonts, and rhynchosaurs (extinct relatives of the lizards); and carnivores from cynodont, thecodontian and early dinosaur stocks. Other dinosaurs ate both plant and animal material and would be termed omnivores. The dicynodonts, characterized by *Dinodontosaurus,* had lost the majority of their teeth; two tusk-like upper canines and a horny beak replacing the normal dentition. *Dinodontosaurus*

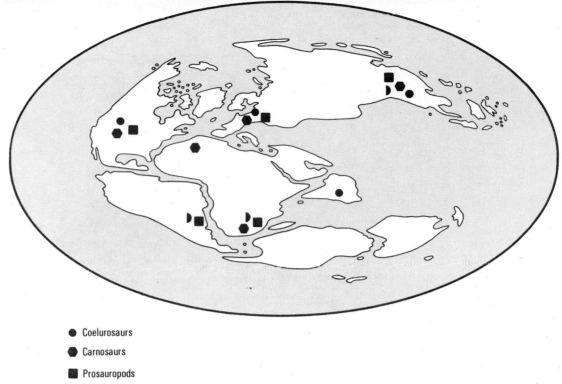

Right Once established, the dinosaurs evolved steadily, numerous forms being found throughout the world by the end of the Triassic Period.

- Coelurosaurs
- Carnosaurs
- Prosauropods
- Ornithischians

spent its life grazing among the soft vegetation bordering rivers, lakes and estuaries. Its plant-eating contemporaries the rhynchosaurs were slightly larger. They possessed a rather parrot-like beak, and hundreds of small teeth covered the jaws and bony palate. Unlike the dicynodonts, the rhynchosaurs probably fed on the seeds and roots of plants that grew some way from the water's edge. It this was so, then it is possible that the predators were similarly deployed. The cynodonts, although very mammal-like in their appearance, were still sprawlers and relied on the slow-moving dicynodonts or their numerous herbivorous cousins (the gomphodont-cynodonts) for food. Thecodontians, such as *Mandasuchus*, lived close to the water's edge feeding on lizards and the occasional dicynodont.

Footprints left in the red muds of the river bank and lakeside, indicate the presence of dinosaurs in the highest levels of the Middle Triassic of South Africa. Some trails were formed by large, heavy quadrupedal creatures

whilst others, much smaller and having three toes, were made by a small bipedal animal. The large animal *Melanorosaurus* lived in lowland areas whilst the small biped, an anchisaur, spent much of its life in the more arid uplands. Both animals were prosauropods. *Melanorosaurus* grew to over 12 metres (39 feet) in length, and its size and great bulk were protection against attack. Its limbs were massively built to support the body weight. It was possible that *Melanorosaurus* spent some of its life in water and occupied a niche similar to that of the great sauropod giants of later times. Anchisaurids on the other hand were smaller, more agile creatures, their bipedal character reminding one of their thecodontian ancestry. *Melanorosaurus* was essentially herbivorous whilst the anchisaurids filled the role of upland predator and scavenger.

Dinosaurs similar to *Melanorosaurus* existed in the Middle Triassic of Argentina, where they shared their environment with the earliest bird-hipped dinosaur *Pisanosaurus*. Small bipedal carnivores such as *Podokesaurus* also flourished in the same region. Other reptiles included the armoured aëtosaurs and other thecodontians. In general terms the fauna was similar to that of southern Africa; other communities in Europe indicate that the earliest ancestral dinosaurs migrated freely. *Melanorosaurus* and various anchisaurids persisted into the Upper Triassic, and evidence for herding is indicated by their relative abundance. As time progressed the climate of the southern African area was to become more arid. Those conditions were more suited to the anchisaurids, and individuals such as *Thecodonto-*

Right Rhynchosaurs such as *Scaphonyx* were common during the Middle Triassic; the parrot-like beak and numerous small teeth on the palate indicate that they feed on tough plant material.

saurus and *Massospondylus* became major components of the fauna. Both were lightly built compared with *Melanorosaurus*, and inhabited a more upland environment. They fed on both plants and meat – ornithischians and even small mammals contributing to their omnivorous diet. Other prosauropods were numerous in these upland regions and the first African coelurosaurs were also present.

During the Upper Triassic the lightly built coelurosaurs were truly widespread, the remains of various species being found in Africa, Asia, Europe and North and South America. In some areas they were really abundant, and in North America (Ghost Ranch, New Mexico) numerous skeletons of the form *Coelophysis* provide information on population structure and mode of life. The skeletons in question were found within a limited 10 metre (33 foot) outcrop, and the suggestion is of sudden catastrophe destroying a family group. Adults and juveniles were found together, with two large individual skeletons having the remains of young within their body cavities. This phenomenon could indicate that these dinosaurs either gave birth to live young, or that adults were cannabalistic. The size of the bones inside the body and the size and shape of the adult pelvis argues against the live birth theory.

In Europe the coelurosaurs were found in association with prosauropods such as *Plateosaurus* and *Plateosauriscus*, and the first of the giant carnosaurs, *Teratosaurus*. The climate was again subtropical with mud-cracks, rain pits and footprints indicating periods of desiccation. Horsetails and lycopsids grew in the wetter lowlands, whilst ferns, conifers, cycads and the rare flowering plants inhabited both lowland and the drier upland regions. Cycads, gingkoes and conifers occurred in greater abundance in the late Triassic, replacing the seed ferns as the prominent plant life. No bird-hipped dinosaurs have been recorded from the Upper Triassic of Europe, and it would appear that the radiation of this group was initially centred in the Southern Hemisphere. The Argentine may have been the place of origin but, by the Upper Triassic, ornithischians were an important element of south African faunas. *Fabrosaurus* and *Heterodontosaurus* lived at the same time as the anchisaurids *Thecodontosaurus* and *Massospondylus*. The ornithischians were strongly bipedal, although *Heterodontosaurus* had quite large front limbs. Both animals were quite small, with *Fabrosaurus* growing to just 1 metre (3 feet) in length. *Fabrosaurus* had a small skull and the teeth were rather unspecialized. *Heterodontosaurus* had differentiated teeth, however, with small incisors, large saw-edged canines and closely packed cheek teeth. When feeding, the animal would clip at the plant material using its small incisors, the food would then be passed on to the cheek teeth which would cut and grind it into fine pieces. *Heterodontosaurus* had muscular jaws, and one can envisage the animal poised on all fours

grinding mouthfuls of 'Mesozoic cud'. The back legs of both *Heterodontosaurus* and *Fabrosaurus* were long and slender, and suggest that they were really fast runners. In view of the number of carnivores that existed at the same time, they needed to be! The long canines of *Heterodontosaurus* could have been used by males during territorial battles.

The two ornithischians of the Upper Triassic, although important, were greatly outnumbered by the saurischian prosauropods and theropods. This bias persists throughout the Jurassic Period although the descendants of *Heterodontosaurus* and *Fabrosaurus* adapted to fill several different niches.

Into the Jurassic

By the beginning of the Jurassic Period the various groups of dinosaurs were firmly established. The prosauropods had vanished, their place being taken by the sauropods, the first of which arose in Triassic times. The early record of Jurassic dinosaurs is limited due to the advance of seas over many lowland areas. Marine sediments dominate the geological record of these times, and the bias in terms of preservation was towards marine organisms. The seas were warm and clear, and abundant molluscs and fishes provided food for aquatic reptiles such as the ichthyosaurs and plesiosaurs. Coral reefs were soon established along the coasts, and sharks and rays hunted the shoals of colourful fishes that lived among the coral mounds. Pterosaurs flew over the seas, frequently diving down to wave level to snatch at fishes swimming close to the surface. Swamps and forests fringed the coastlines but their presence, like that of the dinosaurs, is scantily recorded. From the evidence available the climate of the early Jurassic would appear to have been wetter than that of the Triassic, and the vegetation more luxuriant. In terms of plant types, the flora was essentially the same, except that the conifers, gingkoes and cycads were more widespread. Desert regions still existed in some parts of the world, with the south-western states of North America being a continuation of the arid Triassic landscape.

Dinosaurs appear to have existed in both desert and wetland areas of the Lower Jurassic, with *Dilophosaurus* being found in the Kayenta sandstones of Arizona, and *Scelidosaurus* from marine sediments in the southern coast of England. *Scelidosaurus* lived over 185 million

During the Triassic Period, mammals as well as dinosaurs were to appear in several regions of the world. *Megazostrodon* lived approximately 200 million years ago.

During the Jurassic Period the close proximity of the continental land masses helped dinosaurs migrate from one area to another.

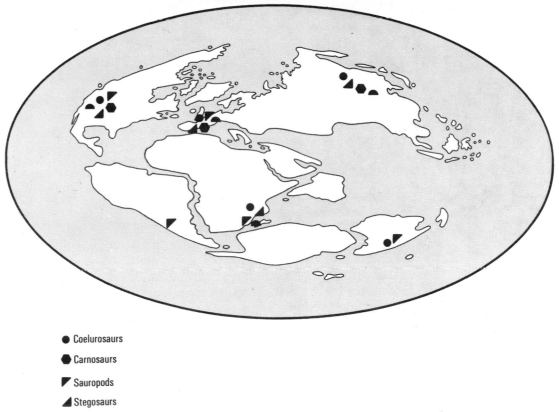

● Coelurosaurs

⬟ Carnosaurs

◤ Sauropods

◢ Stegosaurs

⬤ Ornithopods

years ago and was related to the bipedal ornithischians of the Triassic. It was a quadruped, however, providing proof that although the fossils are absent from the record, the dinosaurs continued to evolve throughout the first half of the Jurassic Period. *Scelidosaurus* was heavily built and slow moving, an easy prey for the great carnosaurs such as *Megalosaurus*. The armour on its back would have offered little protection against attack, but in terms of evolution it was a sign of things to come, as *Scelidosaurus* is regarded as the ancestor of the plated dinosaurs of the Upper Jurassic. The evolution of the dinosaurs during the Middle Jurassic must have been quite spectacular, for the well-preserved faunas of the Upper Jurassic contain many new species.

Apart from the dinosaurs, other groups of reptiles underwent considerable expansion during the Jurassic. These included the crocodiles, lizards and turtles, each of which was to develop marine representation during either the Jurassic or Cretaceous Periods. Together with the dinosaurs these groups replaced ancient stocks such as the pseudosuchian thecodonts, aëtosaurs, phytosaurs and mammal-like reptiles.

Upper Jurassic dinosaurs have been found in many parts of the world, but four areas in particular provide important data related to community structure. The four areas are the western states of North America, the Tendaguru area of Tanzania in East Africa, and southern England and Germany. Geographically these areas were widely separated, but in terms of fauna a number of important comparisons can be made, which suggest that

migration was possible across the various land masses.

In North America the dinosaurs of the Upper Jurassic have been collected from the Morrison sediments of Montana, Wyoming, Utah, Colorado and New Mexico. The extent and variety of these deposits suggest that the animals existed in a setting somewhat similar to that of the Mississippi delta. Tropical and subtropical vegetation dominated, with swamps, thick forests and upland areas providing a number of micro-environments for a varied dinosaur population. Several interpretations exist for the roles of certain animals within this community, and the selection of one theory against another greatly affects the final structure. Essentially the argument centres around the position occupied by the great sauropods, which on fossil evidence account for approximately eighty per cent of the known herbivores.

One theory is that the sauropods such as *Diplodocus, Apatosaurus, Camarosaurus* and *Brachiosaurus* were swamp dwellers. The atlantosaurs (*Diplodocus* and *Apatosaurus*), characterized by short front limbs, are believed to have lived in shallower waters than the camarosaurs (*Brachiosaurus* and *Camarosaurus*) which had long front limbs. In their swampland homes the sauropods would have been safe from attack by the savage carnosaurs – their only contact with *Allosaurus* and *Ceratosaurus* being when they ventured on to land to lay eggs. In the second theory the sauropods are depicted as land dwellers, living a rather giraffe-like existence, browsing on the twigs and needles of tall trees. In this second reconstruction the sauropods would act as the main source of food for the carnosaurs, the predator-prey relationship within the community being similar to that of big cat-herbivore relationship of the African veldt. Unfortunately the actual percentage of animals in the fossil record of the Morrison formation may only reflect the fact that the sauropods died in areas conducive to preservation; whilst the limited representation of carnosaurs and other herbivores, would indicate that the majority of them lived on drier terrain. If this was the case then the carnosaurs could have fed on herds of stegosaurs and camptosaurs with the odd unwary sauropod providing an infrequent source of food. *Stegosaurus, Camptosaurus* and other herbivores account for only fifteen per cent of the herbivores of the Morrison formation.

Apart from the giant sauropods and carnosaurs, other dinosaurs such as the coelurosaurs lived during Morrison times. *Ornitholestes*, the 'bird catcher' was very similar to its Triassic ancestor *Coelophysis* and probably occupied the same niche, preying on small lizards or young dinosaurs. It may also have stolen eggs or scavenged on the carcasses of animals killed by the carnosaurs. *Ornitholestes* was very agile and probably ranged far and wide in its search for food, filling the niche of the jackal and hyaena of the present day.

The fauna of the Tendaguru area of Tánzania was very similar to that of the Morrison formation. *Brachiosaurus* was common to both areas, but *Dicraeosaurus* and *Gigantosaurus* had replaced *Diplodocus* and *Apatosaurus* as the representative atlantosaurs. These great beasts filled the same niches as they did in North America, for the conditions at Tendaguru were remarkably like those present in the western states. Numerically the brachiosaurs appear to have been the most common stock, accounting for over forty per cent of the herbivorous population. The atlantosaurs then accounted for twenty-five per cent whilst *Kentrosaurus*, the faunal equivalent of *Stegosaurus*, made up the majority of the remaining thirty-five per cent. *Kentrosaurus* was a rather spiny version of *Stegosaurus*, with paired spines protecting its back and tail. The tail spines were very long and would have been very useful when the animal was under attack from the resident carnosaurs, *Allosaurus* and *Megalosaurus*. The food chain of Tendaguru was crowned by the presence of the carnosaurs, with the sauropods, stegosaurs and camptosaurs (*Dysalotosaurus*) forming the intermediate links with the plants which are, after all, the primary producers in any community. Peripheral to the chain were the coelurosaurs, which in Africa were represented by the form *Elaphrosaurus*. It is possible that this coelurosaur, like *Ornitholestes*, scavenged on the carcasses left by the carnosaurs and that it shared this role with the pterosaurs that ruled the Upper Jurassic skies.

The pterosaur *Rhamphorhynchus* was common to both East Africa and central Europe (Germany) during the Upper Jurassic. It was a long-tailed pterosaur in which the teeth sloped forward; they appear to have been used to spear fishes which lived in the tropical seas of both areas. In Europe *Rhamphorhynchus* flew over a series of islands and lagoons similar to those found in the tropics of the present day. They shared their aerial domain with the small *Pterodactylus* which, unlike *Rhamphorhynchus*, spent its time catching insects. On the ground the first bird, *Archaeopteryx*, feasted on small basking lizards and on the brightly coloured insects that lived in the low-lying vegetation. *Archaeopteryx* was unable to fly, and was itself in constant danger of attack from coelurosaurs such as *Compsognathus*. Physically there was little to choose between the two animals and it is probable that *Archaeopteryx* and its descendants arose from a coelurosaur ancestor similar to *Compsognathus*. According

Dilophosaurus, the 'two-ridged lizard', was a rather bizarre coelurosaur. The crests may have been sex display structures.

During the Cretaceous Period the positions of the continents were still different from those of today. Dinosaurs were widely distributed.

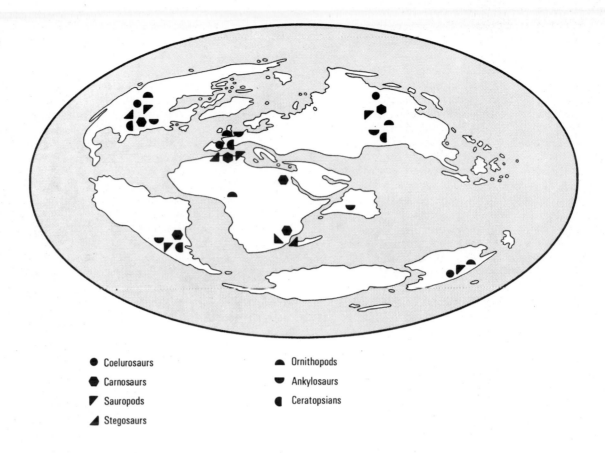

- ● Coelurosaurs
- ⬟ Carnosaurs
- ▼ Sauropods
- ◢ Stegosaurs
- ◖ Ornithopods
- ◡ Ankylosaurs
- ◖ Ceratopsians

to some accounts two species of *Compsognathus* existed during the Upper Jurassic, one having a normal grasping hand, the other a paddle-like structure. The second of these two types was apparently adapted to living part of its life in water, where it hunted shrimps, crabs and a vast spectrum of other invertebrates that thrived in the warm clear waters.

The seas of the Upper Jurassic also covered large areas of northern Europe, and dinosaurs lived along the ancient shoreline that extended through the Midlands of England. Great sauropods like those of North America and East Africa thrived in the lowland swamps, whilst *Megalosaurus* ruled the drier hinterlands. The sauropods were represented by *Cetiosaurus* – the 'whale lizard' – which, like *Brachiosaurus*, had long front limbs. On land the only defences it had against the carnosaurs were its size and whip-like tail. Stegosaurs and iguanodonts were also present in the northern faunas, occupying niches which they were to continue to hold in to the Lower Cretaceous.

Cretaceous dinosaurs

The dawn of the Cretaceous Period was marked by the transgression of the seas over lowland regions. Marine sediments were deposited in many areas where dinosaurs once walked, and the bones and shells of sea-dwelling animals became the diagnostic fossils. Dinosaur localities are known from various sediments during the Early Cretaceous but their number and importance bear little comparison with those of Upper Cretaceous age. Apart from the transgression of the seas, the Lower Cretaceous was in many ways a

continuation of the Upper Jurassic, with the climate remaining warm and wet. In several European areas the landscape was similar to southern Florida, with extensive swamps covering a series of low-lying deltas. Mangrove vegetation covered much of these areas whilst cycads and pines lined the water ways and grew in the higher well-drained areas. Flowering plants occurred in greater numbers than in the Jurassic, and numerous insects were gainfully employed in the gathering of pollen.

Among the dinosaurs, sauropods (including *Cetiosaurus* and *Diplodocus*) still lived in the swamps, and *Megalosaurus* remained the dominant predator. New forms had evolved, however, and *Iguanodon* and *Hypsilophodon* were to herald the rise of the ornithischians as the dominant herbivores of the Cretaceous Period. The iguanodonts were large, bipedal herbivores which browsed among the pines and cycads. They roamed in herds with older, heavier beasts moving around on all four limbs. *Hypsilophodon* was a distant cousin of *Iguanodon*, but unlike 'iguana tooth' it was a very agile creature which has been referred to as the gazelle of the dinosaur world. Both animals lived in the open spaces between woodland areas, sharing their environment with the early armoured dinosaur *Polacanthus*. Unlike its ornithischian relatives *Polacanthus* was relatively slow moving, and to compensate for its lack of speed had developed a spiny dorsal armour. *Iguanodon* and *Hypsilophodon* would have tried to outrun a hungry carnosaur, but *Polacanthus* would crouch low and present its attacker with the almost impossible task of breaking through its spiny body covering.

Marsh turtles, crocodiles, pterosaurs and lizards completed the reptile check list of these areas.

In North America, the Cloverly beds provide additional information on Lower Cretaceous dinosaur communities; the predator-prey ratios making interesting comparison with those of the Jurassic Period. Sauropods accounted for only twenty per cent of the herbivores of this early Cretaceous fauna, whilst the rapidly evolving ornithischians, including the camptosaurs and ankylosaurs, made up the other eighty per cent. Carnosaurs and the fearsome coelurosaur *Deinonychus* were the major predators.

The Lower Cretaceous faunas of Asia compare favourably with those of Europe, with *Iguanodon* being a prominent herbivore. Asia, however, held a few surprises with the ancestors of several ornithischian stocks being found among its early Cretaceous faunas. Included in these was *Psittacosaurus*, a small ornithopod, regarded by many people as the stem from which the horned dinosaurs evolved.

By the Upper Cretaceous a number of great changes were under way which were to affect many aspects of life on this planet. The continents which had been dividing since Triassic times were entering the final stages of division. Two hundred million years ago the supercontinent Pangea had begun to break up, with North America moving away from South America, and a southern split occurring between South America and Africa. By the Lower Cretaceous these rifts had widened and the southern protoatlantic fingered between the last two continents. The drift continued throughout the Cretaceous Period with the southern Atlantic reaching more than half its present width. India split from Australia and Antarctica, and Madagascar broke away from the African continent. Faunal and floral changes accompanied the split of the continents, with the Northern Hemisphere being the centre of evolution for many new species of plant and animal.

The floral changes that took place during the Upper Cretaceous involved the expansion of the flowering plants (angiosperms) into many terrestrial environments. Tropical, subtropical and temperate angiosperm floras can be recognized in the Northern Hemisphere during the late Cretaceous. The temperate flora covered a vast belt of land extending through northeast Europe to Siberia and across part of North America. It consisted mainly of trees and shrubs such as oak, maple, poplar, walnut, hickory, magnolia and viburnum, with some conifers such as the giant sequoia, and gingkoes and ferns. Plants, like animals, spread throughout these northern areas using both the links between Asia and North America, and also between North America, Greenland and Europe as migration routes. The subtropical flora of the late Cretaceous extended northwards as far as southern England, central Russia and Mongolia. A broad arid zone lay to the south of this flora and occupied a tract of land extending from Spain, through North Africa into Asia. It served to separate the subtropical and tropical floras. In the Southern Hemisphere it would appear that one great flora of a rather primitive character covered most areas.

The changes that took place in the composition of dinosaur communities between the Lower and Upper Cretaceous were in response to the floral and geographic changes noted above. In the Northern Hemisphere new families evolved which could live on the new plants, but in the Southern Hemisphere both plants and animals remained archaic. The land links between North America and Asia, across the Bering Straits, and North America, Greenland and Europe allowed the northern faunas to migrate freely, whilst in the south the dinosaurs were to become rather isolated. Sauropods were to remain an important part of the faunas of the Southern Hemisphere whilst the ornithischians were to become the dominant forms in North America and eastern Asia.

The record for these two areas during the Upper Cretaceous is exceptional, with the evidence for population structure and for the existence of interrelationships between dinosaurs reaching hitherto unknown levels. In North America the Upper Cretaceous sediments of Alberta and Montana have yielded vast quantities of dinosaur bones, enabling palaeontologists to reconstruct the environments and the succession of animals that lived in them. The period of time involved was approximately twenty million years, during which at least three distinct dinosaur communities existed in the north-western states. Other communities existed in New Mexico and along the eastern seaboard but their structure is not as well documented as those noted above. The three communities from Montana and Alberta are known after their local names, they are the Belly River, Edmonton and Lance or Hell Creek communities. Of these, the Belly River is the oldest and the lance or Hell Creek the youngest.

Ninety million years ago the Belly River country was essentially a lowland area, the skyline broken only by small hills and the growth of tall oaks and pines. Rivers cut through forests and across open lands, and numerous lakes were dotted over the landscape. The vegetation at the edge of the lakes included palms and magnolia whilst ferns, roses and holly formed the undergrowth in the forests. Small mammals, lizards and snakes lived among this vegetative cover, and birds such as owls perched among the branches. Dinosaurs appeared to be almost everywhere, occupying numerous niches from lake to open plain. The main elements of the fauna were the duck-billed dinosaurs and the ceratopsians, with the heavily armoured ankylosaurs appearing to be a subsidiary stock.

A large variety of duck-billed dinosaurs roamed through the forest glades and across the open plains, with large males at the head of their respective herds. Some hadrosaurs fed near the lakeside with individuals wading into the water to keep cool. The horned dinosaurs also roamed in herds, with short-frilled forms such as *Styracosaurus* and *Monoclonius*, and the long-frilled *Chasmosaurus*, forming distinct populations. Hadrosaurs formed almost seventy per cent of the entire herbivorous stock, the ceratopsians twenty per cent and the ankylosaurs, represented by several forms, another five per cent. The ankylosaurs appear to have succeeded the stegosaurs and, like the ceratopsians, lived on the open lands between forests. In the areas of higher land the first of the dome-headed dinosaurs, or pachycephalosaurs, lived, their herd structure resembling that of the present day mountain sheep or goats. As they were upland creatures, however, their remains were mostly destroyed before preservation was possible, and a true record of their numbers within the community is lost for ever.

Gorgosaurus was the dominant carnosaur of these times, the animal appearing in increased numbers in response to the abundance of herbivorous forms. Like its slightly younger relative *Tyrannosaurus*, *Gorgosaurus* had very small front limbs and only two fingers on each hand. To kill, it would have used its great talon-like feet and large serrated teeth. Other predators lived in the same areas as *Gorgosaurus*, but they were tiny by comparison, and fed on small reptiles and mammals. They were all coelurosaurs, although different individual types occupied a variety of niches. Some, like the dromaeosaurids, had large eyes and relatively large brain cases; they were very agile creatures which searched the undergrowth and rocky crevices for their next prey. Their searches may have been conducted at dusk when the small nocturnal mammals emerged from their daytime hideouts. Other coelurosaurs were more like their ancient ancestor *Coelophysis;* they fed on small lizards and snakes, and on the carcasses left by *Gorgosaurus*. Still others were 'ostrich-like', and *Ornithomimus* filled the role of the egg stealer.

With the march of time, new types of hadrosaurs, ceratopsians and ankylosaurs replaced those of the Belly River formation. The numbers of hadrosaurs were to increase dramatically, with forms such as *Saurolophus* and *Edmontosaurus* and their relatives forming over eighty per cent of the plant-eating population of the Lower Edmonton community. Ceratopsians remained numerous, although *Anchiceratops*, *Pentaceratops* and *Arrhinoceratops* had become the dominant forms. These long-frilled ceratopsians outnumbered the descendants of *Monoclonius*, whilst the 'primitive' *Leptoceratops* appeared to be a throwback from earlier times. Changes in the flora, or fluctuations in the climate, may account for the success of the hadrosaurs which, although spectacular, was relatively short lived. By the end of the Edmonton times, and the emergence of the Lance-Hell Creek community, the hadrosaurs were in decline and vast herds of ceratopsians now roamed the more open landscape of the north-west area of North America.

Horned giants such as *Triceratops* and *Torosaurus* formed half of the plant-eating populations. The anatosaurs had emerged as the main duck-billed stock, but the spectacular forms of earlier times had been replaced by a much less specialized type of animal. This phenomenon is often witnessed in the fossil record and illustrates that animals well suited to stable ecological niches will survive, when other more experimental types vanish with the conditions they thrived in. The evolution of the horned dinosaurs as the major component of the uppermost Cretaceous faunas presented problems for the carnosaurs, for the 8 tonne *Triceratops* was a more difficult animal to kill than the seemingly defenceless hadrosaurs. The carnosaurs' answer was a bigger, more voracious predator than ever known before – *Tyrannosaurus*, an exceedingly powerful killer of gigantic proportions. 'Tyrant lizard' hunted its prey over open plain and through forest glade, and ceratopsians, hadrosaurs and ankylosaurs formed part of its varied diet. *Ornithomimus* continued to fill the role of egg stealer and general scavenger, whilst in the more upland areas *Pachycephalosaurus* represented the evolutionary peak of the dome-headed dinosaurs.

Pachycephalosaurus and its relatives were not confined to North America, and their presence in eastern Asia is evidence for the migration routes mentioned earlier. These had remained open for a long period of time, and faunal comparison reveals that apart from the pachycephalosaurs, hadrosaurs, ceratopsians, 'ostrich-like' coelurosaurs and the carnosaurs were common to both regions. The Djadochta beds of Mongolia have yielded a great deal of information on the early faunas of the Upper Cretaceous. *Protoceratops,* the earliest of the horned dinosaurs, was an important member of the Djadochta community; with dozens of skeletons collected by various expeditions suggesting that the animal lived in herds. It also protected its nests and hatchlings against attacks by the agile coelurosaurs *Oviraptor* and *Velociraptor*. The descendants of *Protoceratops* migrated north-eastwards across the Bering Strait into North America; *Pentaceratops,* the long-frilled ceratopsian, being common to both Asia and to the Edmonton formation of North America.

The first hadrosaur, *Bactrosaurus*, evolved in Mongolia in the Lower Cretaceous; by the Upper Cretaceous its descendants had also crossed the Bering Strait into North America and had spread westwards into Europe. The presence of the ceratopsians in the uppermost Cretaceous of Asia is based on limited evidence, but the evidence for the presence of the hadrosaurs is sufficient to suggest that they were a major component of various reptile communities. Hadrosaurs, ceratopsians and ankylosaurs such as *Pinacosaurus,* probably formed the vast majority of herbivores of the Asian communities, with some sauropods persisting in lowland areas. Carnosaurs such as *Gorgosaurus* and *Tarbo-*

saurus (the Asian equivalent of *Tyrannosaurus*) hunted in many areas. The environment of the Djadochta community is thought to have been terrestrial, with *Protoceratops* and its contemporaries living under rather arid conditions. These differed considerably from those of later times, for the area in which *Tarbosaurus* hunted was characterized by the presence of extensive lakes and great rivers. The time gap between the appearances of *Protoceratops* and *Tarbosaurus* is in the order of twenty million years, the small ceratopsian living 100 million years ago.

Tarbosaurus, like *Tyrannosaurus*, was a very large predator, but it is probable that even more fearsome creatures shared their environments. The great carnosaurs used their back legs and great jaws to subdue their prey; their fore limbs being extremely short and relatively weak. *Deinocheirus*, however, a new type of carnivorous dinosaur, had very long fore limbs which possessed three fingers, each of which terminated in a long hook-like claw. The arms were used to strike and grip the prey, and hands and jaws could be used in savaging the victim's carcass. *Deinocheirus* is known only from the Nemegt Basin of Mongolia, and its presence may indicate that yet another new group of dinosaurs had evolved in this very important area. It is possible that *Deinocheirus* may be found in other lands, but it is also possible that it evolved too late; for by the very end of the Cretaceous, the link between eastern Asia and North America had disappeared. This may account for the confinement of dinosaurs such as *Triceratops* to the North American land mass and may have contributed to the demise of the dinosaurs by the end of the Cretaceous.

Evolutionary trends within the dinosaurs

During the 140 million years that the dinosaurs ruled the earth, hundreds of different types represented various stocks. In some cases the record is extremely poor, but often the material available demonstrates that a number of evolutionary trends took place within this period of time. We can build up a series of ancestor-descendant relationships, and construct a number of family trees that in turn reflect the evolution and radiation of the Dinosauria as a whole. The problems of the ancestry of the group have been dealt with earlier, and it is the evolution of the various suborders, such as the theropods, sauropodomorphs and ornithopods, with which we are concerned here.

The saurischians
In the latter half of the Triassic Period, numerous groups of dinosaurs evolved to occupy a number of ecological niches. Among these were the Prosauropoda which included dino-

saurs of small to moderate size. The majority were semi-quadrupedal, able to move around on either two or four legs. Three family groupings occurred in the Upper Triassic; a typical member of each family representing a stage in the development of the prosauropodian stock. The most 'primitive' individuals appear to have belonged to the anchisaurids, representatives of which have been found in the Americas and South Africa. The forms *Thecodontosaurus* and *Massospondylus*, mentioned earlier, were not the first prosauropods but they do represent less specialized animals. *Thecodontosaurus*, at 2–3 metres (6·5–10 feet) in length was relatively small and lightly built. Its long neck and tail were characteristic of many sauropodomorphs, but its elongate fingers and toes were very different to the great clubbed feet of later forms. *Massospondylus*, of similar design, was almost twice as large as its close relative – the increase in size noted between these anchisaurids being one of the general trends diagnostic of the Sauropodomorpha. *Plateosaurus* and its relatives from Europe and eastern Asia were more advanced than the anchisaurids. They were also much larger, with *Plateosaurus* reaching 8 metres (26 feet) in length. The head was comparatively smaller than that of an anchisaurid, and in general terms it would appear that these animals exhibited a move towards a quadrupedal life style. Their bones had thickened walls, which suggests the need to support a great body weight. The plateosaurids had fairly short digits on the hand, which were spread outwards to give extra support on soft ground. Their feet were still quite long with only the outer toe showing any reduction. Unlike the anchisaurids, *Plateosaurus* had a skull and teeth adapted to a plant-eating diet.

Melanorosaurus was also a plant eater but, unlike *Plateosaurus*, it exhibited little or no evidence of ever being bipedal. Its massive limbs supported a great body weight; the animal attaining a length of some 12 metres (39 feet). *Melanorosaurus* represented the culmination of prosauropod evolution and was probably ancestral to the later sauropods. It had massive limbs, with long, solid bones, and a strongly constructed backbone. The heavy nature of the lower skeleton and the development of neck vertebrae, in which hollowed areas reduced the overall weight, separated *Melanorosaurus* from other prosauropod stocks. A small head and shortened, elephant-like feet also indicate that this dinosaur was a lowland swamp dweller. The increase in size shown by the prosauropods protected them from the more agile theropods, but forced them to adopt a semi-aquatic mode of life to support their increased bulk.

Most palaeontologists believe that this was the life style also adopted by the sauropods, which at first sight would have appeared as simple enlargements of *Melanorosaurus*-type animals. The earliest recorded sauropods belong to the camarosaur or brachiosaur family, in which individuals are characterized

The sauropods were the largest dinosaurs. Two distinct lines of evolution represented the family during the Jurassic and Cretaceous Periods.

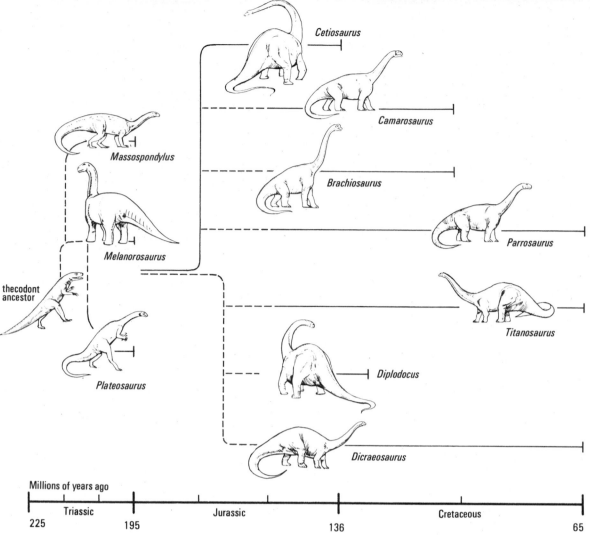

Millions of years ago

| Triassic | Jurassic | Cretaceous |

225   195   136   65

by having front legs which are longer than the back legs. *Rhoetosaurus* from the Lower Jurassic of Australia and *Cetiosaurus* from the Middle Jurassic of Europe, were the earliest camarosaurs. Representatives of the second family, the atlantosaurs, did not appear until the Upper Jurassic; their absence in early faunas being problematic but not unexplainable. The problem is one of origin, with two or more solutions being available from the evidence in the fossil record. One solution is that both groups evolved from a common ancestor such as *Melanorosaurus*, but because of the poor record of faunas in the Lower and Middle Jurassic, the earliest atlantosaurs remain undiscovered. The second solution would involve the evolution of the atlantosaurs from an early camarosaur in Middle Jurassic times. In both cases the origin of the two groups represents a basic subdivision within the sauropods, and the successful occupation of different ecological niches.

Apart from the differences in the lengths of the front limbs between the two groups, other changes affected the shape and structure of the skull and the number of teeth. In camarosaurs, such as *Camarosaurus* and *Brachiosaurus*, the skull was rather deep and proportionately larger than that of *Diplodocus* or *Apatosaurus*.

The camarosaurs also had numerous peg-like teeth along the margins of the jaws, whilst the trend in the atlantosaurs was towards the concentration of the teeth into the anterior area of the mouth. This trend would indicate that *Diplodocus* and its relatives spent their life plucking at leaves and gathering soft vegetation that grew along the banks of their swampland home. *Brachiosaurus* on the other hand lived in deeper waters, breathing through nostrils placed high on the head, as it fed with its neck stretched out of the surface of the water.

The largest sauropods represented a spectacular development from their prosauropod ancestors; registering a 200-fold increase in weight and a 15-fold increase in length. Size enabled the sauropods to shrug off the threat of the ever-present carnosaurs and to survive for over ninety million years. In terms of Man, this was the equivalent of 3,600,000 generations.

According to some palaeontologists the prosauropods and sauropods can be traced back to theropod ancestors, with the small coelurosaurs acting as the base stock for the radiation of all saurischian dinosaurs. The theropods were the 'beast-footed' saurischians, representatives of which were present through-

28

out the Age of Reptiles. In the late Triassic the two groups of theropods, the coelurosaurs and carnosaurs, were already present, with the small coelurosaurs appearing to be the more primitive of the two. Early representatives of this stock appear to be very similar, with *Coelophysis* being regarded as the common ancestor for all later forms. Throughout their history the coelurosaurs were to remain relatively small creatures which, as we have seen, were well equipped to fill the role of scavenger or predator on small animals. Like many of their thecodontian ancestors they were bipedal with a lightly built frame and thin-walled bones. At first they were all predators, but as time progressed new families appeared which had lost their predatory habits. Some individuals, such as *Ornitholestes* and *Velociraptor*, were to indicate that the typical predatory stock continued throughout Jurassic and Cretaceous times. These more advanced forms were to show a reduction in the number of fingers and toes in the hands and feet; the grasping power of the hand increasing with time.

During the early Cretaceous, a new group of coelurosaurs, the 'ostrich-like' dinosaurs, appeared in North America. They retained the bipedal posture of their cousins but were characterized by a smaller head and the loss of teeth. Forms such as *Ornithomimus* and *Oviraptor* were even more lightly built than their ancestors, having the general proportions of the ostrich, with which they are often compared. Their heads were very bird-like, the teeth being replaced by a horny beak. Both hands and feet possessed three digits, with the hands retaining the grasping function of earlier forms. The evolution of the ornithomimids was towards an animal which was extremely fleet of foot, with hands that could lift and hold eggs. They became the egg stealers of the Upper Cretaceous, their long legs giving them great speed with which they avoided the angry parents from whose nests they stole.

The ornithomimids and the normal predatory coelurosaurs were daytime feeders. They robbed nests or hunted small reptiles in forest glades and along the edges of the swamps. At night, whilst they rested, the furry mammals emerged from their hiding places in the hope that the fading light would protect them from attack. By the end of the Lower Cretaceous, however, the coelurosaurs had evolved to fill this new niche, and individuals with large brains and enormous eyes had evolved to hunt and kill in the low light of dusk. These were the dromaeosaurids, a branch of coelurosaurs which, according to some palaeontologists, represented the climax of dinosaur evolution. They apparently possessed an intelligence similar to that of birds, with the brain accounting for 1/1000th of the body weight. (In the sauropods the brain accounted for approximately 1/100,000th of the body weight, and a comparison of the two figures quickly reveals the lack of functional prowess in the cumbersome swamp dwellers.) The trends within the coelurosaurs were to include the increase in brain size noted above, and a general increase in the size of individual forms. This was in no way comparable with that described for the Sauropodomorpha, and would suggest that the coelurosaurs were well adapted to their particular mode of life from the outset.

The evolution of the giant carnosaurs ran parallel with that of their small cousins, with various individuals exhibiting a number of changes to their flesh-eating and hunting habits. As with the other Saurischia, the most obvious trend was that of an increase in overall size – *Tyrannosaurus* representing a 4- or 5-fold increase over its Triassic ancestors. The depth of the skull also increased, and the gape of the jaws reached frightening proportions in certain individuals. In early forms the teeth could be described as fairly large, whilst later forms were armed with huge serrated structures. These modifications of the teeth and jaws enabled the animals to tear great lumps of meat from a carcass and to bolt the lumps down into the stomach. Giants such as *Gorgosaurus* and *Tyrannosaurus* needed a great deal of food to survive, and it would appear logical that the

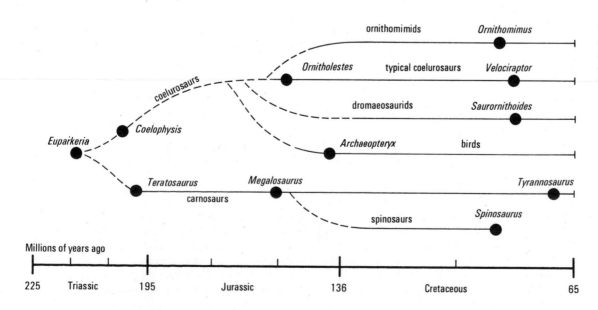

The coelurosaurs and carnosaurs represent two distinct lines of evolution within the Theropoda, or 'beast-footed' dinosaurs.

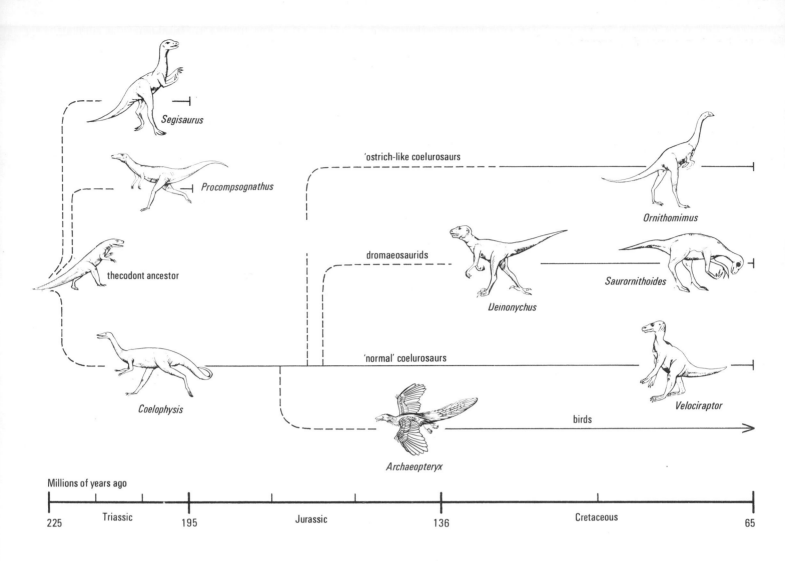

'ostrich-like coelurosaurs'

dromaeosaurids

'normal' coelurosaurs

thecodont ancestor

Segisaurus

Procompsognathus

Coelophysis

Deinonychus

Archaeopteryx

Ornithomimus

Saurornithoides

Velociraptor

birds

Millions of years ago

225 — Triassic — 195 — Jurassic — 136 — Cretaceous — 65

The coelurosaur family tree. The history of the group is well documented, and their presence throughout the Age of Dinosaurs is an indication of their success.

differences between them and their ancestors were adaptations related to feeding and hunting. Apart from improvements in the teeth and the jaw mechanism, changes in the length of the neck, the size of the fore limbs and the structure of the foot also took place.

Each modification improved both the balance of the animal and its ability to attack and kill large, often fleet-footed plant eaters. As mighty hunters the carnosaurs needed speed and strength; large fore limbs and broad flat feet would have only hindered their movements. The evolution of the carnosaurs is often seen as a simple progression towards larger and larger forms. To some extent this view is correct, but the emergence of the spinosaurids in the Cretaceous would indicate that even the carnosaurs were quite adventurous; these large, sail-backed meat eaters representing an adaptation to different climatic conditions. *Spinosaurus*, of the Cretaceous of Egypt, lived on the edge of a large tract of arid country. The climate was tropical, and the large sail enabled it to survive in conditions where its flat-backed relatives would literally have boiled. The spread of the spinosaurids into this barren region was governed by the availability of food, and it is probable that, as with giant carnosaurs evolving to eat giant herbivores, sail-backed predators evolved to feed on sail-backed plant eaters. The evidence for this is tentative, but *Ouranosaurus*, the 'heavenly lizard', does exhi-

bit similar adaptations within the same geographic region. *Ouranosaurus* is but one example of the adaptive radiation that took place within the Ornithischia during the Age of Reptiles.

The ornithischians

As with the 'lizard-hipped' dinosaurs, the general trend within all the various stocks of the Ornithischia is towards an increase in size. Other adaptations, however, enabled different forms to successfully occupy a wide variety of ecological niches throughout the world. The first ornithischians, such as *Pisanosaurus*, *Heterodontosaurus* and *Fabrosaurus*, were quite small. All were bipedal, although *Heterodontosaurus* probably walked on all four legs in search of food. It could manipulate its hands, and had powerful arms. *Heterodontosaurus* was also capable of 'mincing' or chopping its food into fine pieces, and in some ways it appeared more specialized towards its plant-eating life style than did later forms such as *Camptosaurus* and *Iguanodon*.

These last two forms represented the main evolutionary line from *Fabrosaurus*, with *Camptosaurus* being five times as long as its ancestor, and *Iguanodon* ten times as long. *Camptosaurus* was the earlier and more primitive of these two ornithopods. It was strongly bipedal although the arms remained stout, with

30

the hands having a full complement of fingers. Like its ancestors, it had muscular cheeks which allowed it to take in a large amount of food at one time. Unlike cows or sheep, *Camptosaurus* could not chew its food, and the muscular cheeks helped to push the plant material into the area between the teeth. These occurred in a single row in the cheek region, their scissor-like action chopping and slicing the food into small fragments. The front of the mouth was toothless, and it is thought that *Camptosaurus* used its tongue and beak to pull and pluck from low branches and for browsing among the undergrowth.

Iguanodon, from the Lower Cretaceous of Europe, was almost twice the size of *Camptosaurus*. Its head was proportionately larger and there was a noticeable increase in body bulk. The teeth and beak were similar, however, and it is probable that it lived in much the same way as its North American ancestor. Unlike *Camptosaurus*, *Iguanodon* had developed a pointed, spike-like thumb as a defensive weapon against any potential attacker. Coupled with an increase in size, the thumb must have made *Iguanodon* look a much more formidable opponent than perhaps it was. *Iguanodon* lived in a wet, subtropical climate, whilst its close relative *Ouranosaurus* existed in an arid, tropical region.

The main line of ornithopod evolution persisted throughout the Jurassic and Cretaceous. In itself it was unspectacular, but it was to act as the stem stock from which several very specialized groups were to evolve. The first of these was to include *Hypsilophodon* and its close relatives which, according to some authors, were among the most primitive ornithopods ever known. In fact, *Hypsilophodon* was often depicted as a tree dweller, perched high in the branches out of reach of any likely predator. This reconstruction was wrong, however, and recent studies of the skeleton of the Cretaceous plant eater show that it was one of the fastest dinosaurs to have lived on Earth.

Unlike *Iguanodon*, *Hypsilophodon* remained small and rather compact, relying on speed and agility to survive in a highly competitive community. It was strongly bipedal unlike *Psittacosaurus*, a rather unique ornithopod from the Cretaceous of Mongolia.

Psittacosaurus, the 'parrot lizard', was over twice the length of *Hypsilophodon,* and rather bulky in appearance. It was able to move around on either two or four legs in search of the succulent palms that formed the basis of its diet. The front of the mouth was like the beak of a parrot, and the back of the head showed signs of a small frill. These features were exactly what one would look for in the search for an ancestor of the horned dinosaurs. Unfortunately, *Psittacosaurus* had fewer finger bones than its would-be descendants, and it is possible that it represented only an interesting experiment in the evolution of the ceratopsians.

Mongolia was the breeding ground for many new families during the early Cretaceous, and it was there that the first duck-billed dinosaur appeared just over 100 million years ago. It evolved from a medium-sized iguanodont ancestor and was to form the stem, or starting point, for one of the most spectacular groups of Upper Cretaceous dinosaurs. The earliest recorded hadrosaur is *Bactrosaurus* from the Lower Cretaceous of Mongolia, but whether it was the first of the line is open to question. Geologically speaking, it occurs in the right place at the right time, but its teeth and limbs may indicate that it was already too advanced. Another early form, *Claosaurus* from North America, occurred slightly later in time than *Bactrosaurus*, but its size and the nature of its teeth and feet suggest that it represented a primitive stage in the development of the group. *Claosaurus*, at 3 metres (10 feet), was

The carnosaur family tree. Their thecodont ancestry and close relationship with the coelurosaurs are clearly indicated.

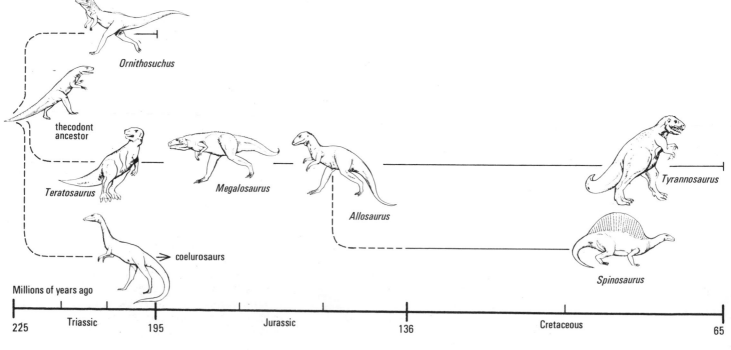

Ornithosuchus

thecodont ancestor

Teratosaurus

Megalosaurus

Allosaurus

coelurosaurs

Tyrannosaurus

Spinosaurus

Millions of years ago

225   Triassic   195   Jurassic   136   Cretaceous   65

only one-third the size of later hadrosaurs, and its teeth were less complicated. It also possessed the vestiges of the first toe present on the hind foot, as did its iguanodont ancestors. It is likely that *Claosaurus* was an intermediate form along the line of evolution that led from the iguanodonts to the hadrosaurs; it also provides evidence for the migration of the duck-billed dinosaurs on to the North American land mass. The skulls and jaws of both *Bactrosaurus* and *Claosaurus* are known only from fragmentary evidence, and therefore it is impossible to state their relative positions in the evolutionary line with absolute certainty, or to comment on whether either was crested or flat headed.

Approximately seventy-five million years ago, both flat-headed and crested hadrosaurs were abundant in various regions of the Northern Hemisphere. The most spectacular collection of different types has been recorded from western North America, and it is from this region that one can begin to reconstruct the complex family tree of the group. The most primitive stock present were the kritosaurs which, like all hadrosaurs, had a body similar to that of the iguanodonts, except that the hands were webbed, the feet hoof-like and the tail stiffer and more flattened. These features are somewhat contradictory within one animal, for whilst the hoofed feet suggest that the hadrosaurs were upland dwellers, the webbed fingers and flattened tail indicate some aquatic specialization. Naturally one could assume that these animals were equally at home in either environment, using their hands and tail to swim across lakes and avoid attack. The kritosaurs were flat-headed hadrosaurs which had a narrow face and facial hump, or plate. In *Kritosaurus* a hump was found in front of the eyes, whilst in the more advanced *Brachylophosaurus* the face bones had grown backwards to form a thick, protective plate. These facial developments are interpreted as weapons used in territorial battles and it is possible that they were less well developed in female animals. Fighting is regarded as a primitive function among the hadrosaurs, and the development within separate families of crests or broad bills, represents a trend away from physical contact, and towards intimidatory displays. *Kritosaurus* also possessed an inflatable organ in the front part of the snout which could change in size and colour. This organ would attract attention to the facial hump and perhaps deter any intruder, be it another male or potential predator. In *Brachylophosaurus* the flattened head plate was used during territorial battles, when males would push and strike each other in a test of strength.

Several more specialized stocks arose from the primitive kritosaur type; the saurolophines representing one distinct trend. In various skulls the display organ and facial hump became integrated, with the result that inflation and colour change would make the face structures seem larger than they actually were. Display alone would then be sufficient to deter any young interloper from challenging a mature male for his harem. In *Prosaurolophus*

The ornithopods flourished during the Cretaceous Period. Their ancestry has been traced back to animals such as *Fabrosaurus* from the Triassic of southern Africa.

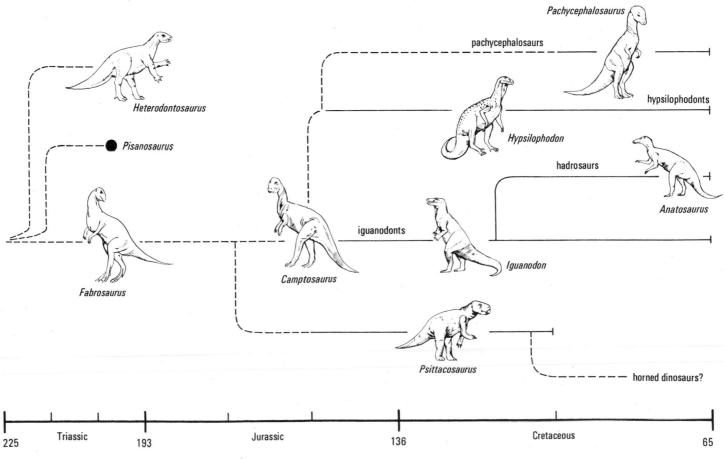

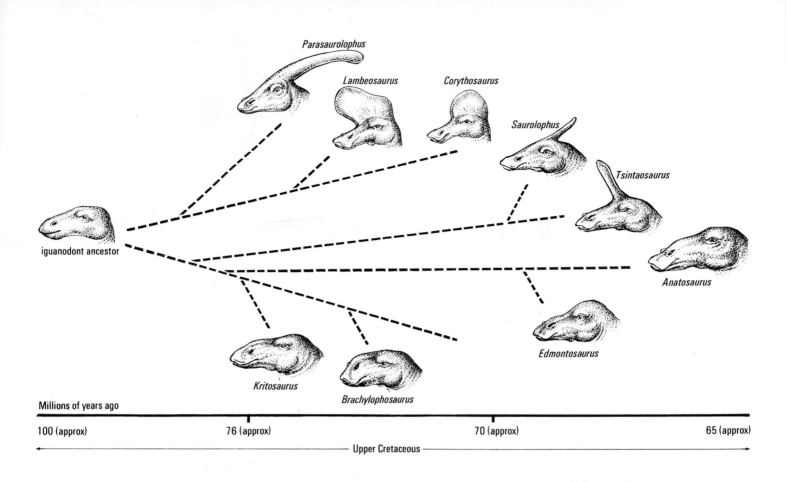

Parasaurolophus

Lambeosaurus   Corythosaurus

Saurolophus

Tsintaosaurus

iguanodont ancestor

Anatosaurus

Edmontosaurus

Kritosaurus

Brachylophosaurus

Millions of years ago

100 (approx)   76 (approx)   70 (approx)   65 (approx)

Upper Cretaceous

the nasal bones formed a small crest, which was to increase considerably in *Saurolophus*. The crest supported a frill which, through the intake of air along complex and elongate nasal passageways, could be inflated as part of the display mechanism. In an area where many animals of similar appearance lived, the feature could be used for identification.

In the Upper Cretaceous, the regions where the hadrosaurs lived, were a mixture of open lands and forests, with lakes and swamps dotting the lowland landscape. Different groups of duck-billed dinosaurs occupied different niches, with the crested and 'hump-snouted' varieties living on the plains where their display mechanisms and features could have more value. Others, such as the edmontosaurs, lacked either crest or hump and are thought to have been forest dwellers.

Individuals such as *Edmontosaurus* and *Anatosaurus,* developed broad, spoon-like beaks, with those of the males being much larger than those of juvenile or female animals. The function of the broad beak is difficult to explain, but as it was coupled with a large increase in the size of the nasal passageways, it could be that these animals made sounds and that this was their method of communication and the way in which they defined their respective territories. This vocalization could be compared with the bellowing of crocodiles and alligators in the modern-day swamplands of Florida. In some ways the edmontosaurs could be regarded as a more basic group, showing none of the crest specializations of the lambeosaurines.

The latter form a distinct group within the

hadrosaurs, each member possessing a prominent crest above the orbits. Unlike the edmontosaurs, they had a narrow face which was formed by the elongate premaxillary bones. These also formed part of the crest which in *Parasaurolophus* was twice the length of the skull. The posterior region of the crest was formed by the nasal bones. Lambeosaurines such as *Parasaurolophus, Lambeosaurus* and *Corythosaurus* were spectacular creatures, the crests of the different sexes and age groups giving some idea of the rank structure that existed in Upper Cretaceous herds. The crests were mainly used as signal structures, although it is probable that the bellowing of large males was also heard within lambeosaurine ranks. A recent study of the various hadrosaur stocks in western North America, has indicated that the rates of evolution in these Upper Cretaceous forms was quite rapid. It also revealed that many of the smaller species previously identified by earlier workers were in fact juveniles or females of larger forms. Because of this, genera such as *Cheneosaurus* have been removed from our family tree, their known remains being incorporated under the name of their likely adult species.

In detail the study confirms that the hadrosaurs evolved as an advanced offshoot from the iguanodont lineage; large numbers of skeletons throughout the Upper Cretaceous being preserved as a testimony to their success. In their terrestrial environment the hadrosaurs developed into large herds, the structure and behaviour of the herds and of individuals being determined by the sexual selection which took place within adult populations. In this way

The family tree of the hadrosaurs, the most successful group of ornithopod dinosaurs.

certain features became common within breeding populations. These features were in themselves adaptations to a certain mode of life. The development of crests and beaks were an intimate part of the selection process, and they undoubtedly played a role in the evolution of the hadrosaurs.

Another advanced offshoot from the iguanodont line were the pachycephalosaurs of the Upper Cretaceous of North America, Europe and Mongolia. Compared with other ornithopods they were rather small creatures, which resembled *Hypsilophodon* in the form of their bodies. They probably arose in late Jurassic times, but the first representative, *Stegoceras,* is known from the uppermost Cretaceous of western North America. Its skull was only 19 centimetres (7·5 inches) long, but the bone

history of the pachycephalosaurs, like that of several other ornithopod families, is relatively short, geologically speaking. Their appearance and extinction within the span of several million years reflects, in part, the explosion of the ornithischian dinosaurs during the Cretaceous.

Apart from the Ornithopoda, other groups of 'bird-hipped' dinosaurs formed important elements of various Mesozoic communities. They exhibited a number of evolutionary trends which in many ways rivalled the spectacular developments of the hadrosaur and pachycephalosaur stocks. These animals were quadrupedal, with the first group, the Stegosauria, spanning some sixty million years of geological time. The first known stegosaur is *Scelidosaurus* from the Lower Jurassic of

Our reconstruction of the ankylosaur family tree suggests that two stocks – the nodosaurs and acanthopholids – evolved side-by-side during the Cretaceous Period.

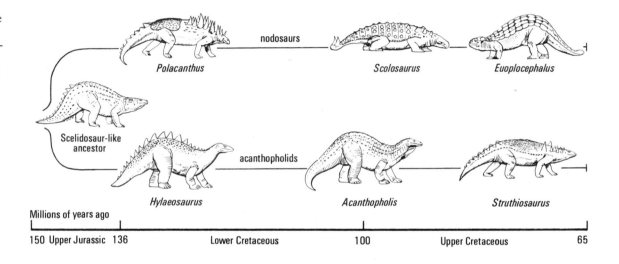

over the brain case was four or five times as thick as that of a man's. In mammals such as mountain goats or sheep a thickening of the skull, especially in males, is primarily linked with butting and dominance. These functions are now attributed to the domes of the pachycephalosaurs with *Stegoceras* representing an early stage in the evolution of the group. In *Pachycephalosaurus* the dome was considerably thicker (22 centimetres or 8·7 inches) and surrounded by a ring of spikes and small knobs of bone. The skull itself was also much larger than that of *Stegoceras,* measuring over 60 centimetres (2 feet) from the tip of the snout to the back of the head. This is a 4-fold increase in size and, coupled with the elaboration of the dome, represents the main evolutionary trends within the family.

As only the skulls of *Pachycephalosaurus* have been discovered, it is likely that after the animals died the climatic conditions that prevailed were such that the more delicate postcranial skeleton was broken up and destroyed. Such conditions prevail in arid upland areas where heat and decay act as agents to rot the flesh; the skeleton gradually falls apart and a sudden downpour will separate the individual bones. The skull of the pachycephalosaurs was heavy and probably not transported as far as the lighter ribs and limb bones. The recorded

Dorset, England. It was approximately 4 metres (13 feet) long, with the body protected by a thick armour of bony plates. *Scelidosaurus* was ancestral to beasts such as *Stegosaurus* and *Kentrosaurus* which were considerably larger, and armoured in spectacular fashion. The increase in size was a trend common to most dinosaur stocks but the development of a spiny or plated armour was specific to this group. In *Kentrosaurus* the plates and spines appeared to have had a mainly defensive role, protecting the animal against attack from a giant carnosaur. In *Stegosaurus,* however, the plates are now thought to have played an important role in the regulation of the body temperature – their positions on the back of the animal and their individual shapes being supported by evidence of an increased blood supply into their central areas.

The stegosaurs were initially lowland dwellers, but as time progressed and they increased in size, they migrated into upland niches. The bones of *Scelidosaurus* were much lighter than those of its descendants and its feet less hooflike. In *Stegosaurus* and *Kentrosaurus* the trends towards more solid limb bones and hoof-like feet reached their climax and it is probable that these were adaptations to an upland mode of life. During the Upper Jurassic and early part of the Lower Cretaceous, the stegosaurs were among the most successful ornithischian stocks. In the Cretaceous their role was gradually assumed by the Ankylosauria which were to reach their evolutionary climax in the Upper Cretaceous.

According to some authorities, the ankylosaurs and stegosaurs shared a common ancestry, with both groups evolving from *Scelidosaurus*. An alternative view is that the ankylosaurs were an offshoot from the stegosaur lineage. Some early forms, such as *Syrmosaurus* from the Lower Cretaceous of Mongolia, exhibit a mixture of stegosaur and nodosaur characters and may represent the intermediate condition between the two stocks. Other Lower Cretaceous forms indicate that early division occurred within the ankylosaurs; with one family, the acanthopholids, retaining many rather primitive features, whilst the other, the nodosaurids, represented the more advanced condition. *Acanthopholis* lived at about the same time as *Syrmosaurus,* but in the south of England. It was just 4 metres (13 feet) in length and heavily built, the hind legs being rather massive structures. The body was covered with a flexible armour of bony plates, and rows of small spines covered the neck area. It lacked the heavy skull armour of later ankylosaurs and had a rather long head and slender body. *Acanthopholis* was ancestral to *Struthiosaurus* which lived in Europe during the Upper Cretaceous.

Struthiosaurus, like its ancestor, had a small head which was less depressed than that of the better-known nodosaurs. It also lacked their heavy cranial armour, but like all late ankylosaurs it had developed a body cover of bony plates and spines. *Struthiosaurus* was characterized by the presence of two very large spines over the shoulder area and two rows of vertical plates that ran from the hips to the tip of the tail. Although they survived for a long period of time, the record of the acanthopholids is poor when compared with that of their nodosaurid cousins.

Polacanthus, of southern England, was the first of the nodosaurids, and it lived during the Lower Cretaceous. In some ways it resembled *Struthiosaurus,* for it had a small head and very large spines over the front part of the body. The latter was broader and flatter, however, and the neck much shorter. *Polacanthus* seemed to reflect the stegosaurian method of defensive armour, whilst its descendants developed a heavy body covering of closely linked plates. Upper Cretaceous nodosaurs were generally larger than *Polacanthus,* with their heavy bodies held closer to the ground. Their heads were larger and a bony helmet often covered the dorsal region. All the evolutionary trends within the nodosaurs appear to have been linked to the successful occupation of an upland niche, and their protection within it. Apart from the development of cranial and body armour the later nodosaurs had fused ribs and vertebrae, which must have added to the strength of the animal. Unlike earlier forms, animals such as *Euoplocephalus* and *Scolosaurus* developed a club-like tail. This could indicate either territorial battling among males or the need for a defensive weapon against the marauding carnosaurs. The trends noted above were obviously successful, as the nodosaurs formed an important element within dinosaur communities until the end of the Cretaceous Period.

The final group of ornithischians to be considered are the ceratopsians, many of which rank among the best known of all the dinosaurs. They spanned some thirty million years of geological time and exhibited a number of evolutionary trends. The evolution of the horned dinosaurs began in the Upper Cretaceous with an ornithopod similar to *Psittacosaurus* representing the ancestral or intermediate form. *Protoceratops* was the first true ceratopsian, the diagnostic frill extending well back over the neck and shoulders. Unlike *Psittacosaurus, Protoceratops* was quadrupedal. The increase in the size of the frill in *Protoceratops* was disproportionate with the increase in the size of the body, for although *Protoceratops* was the same overall size as *Psittacosaurus,* its frill accounted for almost half the length of the skull. Strangely the development of the frill in the life cycle of the individual protoceratopsian also followed a similar pattern, with that of the adult being proportionately much larger than that of the hatchling. This type of phenomenon is a common occurrence and indicates that the development of the individual often reflects the evolution of the group.

Protoceratops was the common ancestor for all horned dinosaur stocks, the great radiation of the group taking place approximately eighty million years ago. Three main lines of ceratopsians arose from *Protoceratops*, with the small *Leptoceratops* representing the central ancestral strain. In fact *Leptoceratops* was a 'throw back' to the days of *Psittacosaurus,* for it had a flat crest instead of a frill and was probably semi-bipedal. The small *Montanoceratops* supposedly continued the *Protoceratops-Leptoceratops* line, but unlike either of these animals it was endowed with a well-developed horn on its nose. These small ceratopsians failed to survive into the uppermost Cretaceous.

The two main branches of the ceratopsians are commonly known as the long-crested and short-crested types; most vertebrate palaeontologists believing that the long-crested branch diverged from the short-crested stock somewhere along the line linking *Protoceratops* with *Monoclonius*. The initial development in both stocks was one of size increase, with the short-crested *Monoclonius* and the long-crested *Chasmosaurus* being several times the length of *Protoceratops*. This initial increase was quite dramatic; later developments in size being of a more gradual nature. In the short-crested ceratopsians, the nose horn showed a varied development, being large in *Monoclonius* and *Styracosaurus,* but short in *Triceratops*. The brow horns, on the other hand, were poorly developed in the first two genera but assumed massive proportions in *Triceratops*.

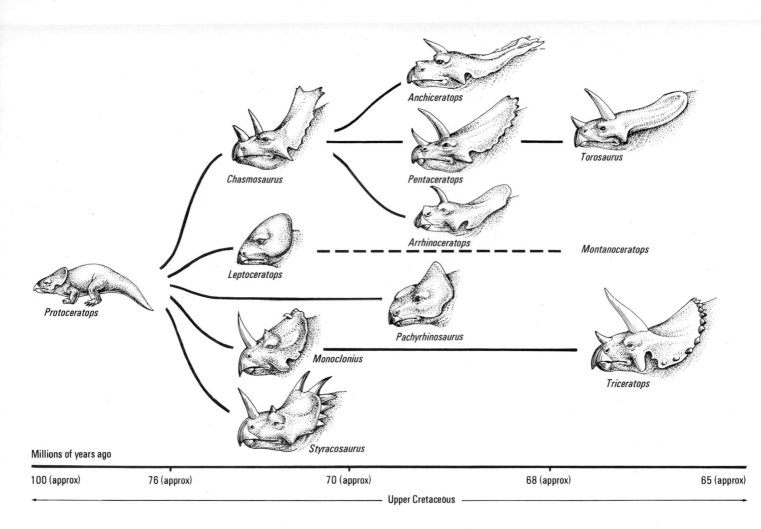

Chasmosaurus

Anchiceratops

Pentaceratops

Torosaurus

Arrhinoceratops

Montanoceratops

Leptoceratops

Protoceratops

Pachyrhinosaurus

Monoclonius

Triceratops

Styracosaurus

Millions of years ago

| 100 (approx) | 76 (approx) | 70 (approx) | 68 (approx) | 65 (approx) |

Upper Cretaceous

The family tree of the horned dinosaurs. During the Upper Cretaceous several distinct lineages evolved.

Styracosaurus was a contemporary of *Monoclonius*, but its exceedingly small brow horns and the spiky nature of its frill exclude it from the direct line of evolution; its limited appearance in the geological record suggesting that it was a spectacular but unsuccessful experiment. The culmination of the short-crested lineage was *Triceratops horridus* which, according to some authorities, showed a 5-fold increase in length and a 9-fold increase in weight over its ancestor *Protoceratops*. *Triceratops* was represented in the uppermost Cretaceous by numerous species, which in two or three million years exhibited several evolutionary trends. The first species occurred in the Edmonton Formation of western North America, but during the succeeding Lance Formation no less than ten species roamed across the North American landscape. In the comparatively short period of time noted above, evolutionary developments were to bring about an overall increase in size of body and changes in the detail of the skull. Like the body, the skull was to show a considerable increase in size, with the crests of the more advanced species being broader than those of primitive ones. In species such as *T. albertensis* and *T. serratus*, the crest was relatively narrow and the nose horn quite large; whilst in *T. horridus* and *T. eurycephalus* the crest was broad and the nose horn much reduced. The last two species also showed a considerable increase in the size of the brow horns; these structures obviously becoming the main weapons for defence. It is possible

that, as in the hadrosaurs, some of the species referred to *Triceratops* were actually males and females of the same stock.

In the case of the long-crested ceratopsians, a greater number of genera have been collected from the Upper Cretaceous sediments of western North America. These genera, to some extent, paralleled the developments described for the short-crested types, with an overall increase in the sizes of head and body being the main developments. The nose horn also appeared to diminish whilst the length of the brow horns increased considerably. In *Pentaceratops* and *Torosaurus* the crest attained truly enormous proportions, covering the neck and much of the back of the animal with a strong bony armour. In the earliest ceratopsians the frill was essentially developed to serve as an area of attachment for the powerful jaw muscles. This function was to remain of major importance throughout the history of the group, but in later forms its protective role was increased considerably.

Other trends visible in the ceratopsians as a group included a reduction in the length of the tail, the development of hoof-like feet and an increase in the massiveness of the hind limbs. All of these developments made the horned dinosaurs particularly suited to an upland mode of life. They occurred in great herds and spread throughout much of the Northern Hemisphere, with *Triceratops* surviving as long as any known species of dinosaur. It is strange that a world which had encouraged the rapid development of this group, should change so quickly as to cause their complete and utter extinction.

The dinosaurs vanish

Fossils of dinosaurs are unknown from rocks deposited after the end of the Cretaceous Period. Beasts such as *Triceratops* and *Tyrannosaurus* had vanished without trace, the last dinosaur bones occurring in rocks over sixty-five million years old. The group ruled the earth for 140 million years, with many types evolving to occupy a wide variety of ecological niches. Some were gigantic but others were small, and many may have been warm-blooded. As individuals and as a group they had dominated the agile, warm-blooded and intelligent mammals since the Triassic; but it was to this group that the dinosaurs left their world.

In earlier times the demise of a group of animals such as the amphibians or the thecodontians could be linked with the evolution of a more advanced stock; the new animals being better suited to the prevailing conditions, or equipped with some new feature which would make them superior to their contemporaries. In this way the dinosaurs had proved to be more efficient than their thecodontian ancestors and had replaced them as the dominant reptilian stock by the end of the Triassic. At the end of the Cretaceous, however, the mammals were still rather insignificant creatures; they were small and mostly insectivorous – hardly the animals one would expect to challenge and replace the dinosaurs. In fact the real radiation of the Mammalia did not take place until several million years after the extinction of the dinosaurs, and therefore the picture of agile mammals raiding reptile nests and causing the extinction of the 'terrible lizards' commands little support. The extinction is, however, indelibly recorded in the fossil record, and this great mystery has been much studied by scientists.

The explanations for the disappearance of the dinosaurs are numerous and include some bizarre, even incredulous ideas. Some, like the great flood or a lack of standing room in Noah's Ark, have a biblical flavour, whilst others including mass suicides and dinosaur wars support the cinema image of the group. Numerous illnesses and diseases have also been suggested, with slipped discs and a reduction in the size of the brain supporting the popular conception that all dinosaurs were enormous, rather pitiful creatures.

The more scientific arguments for extinction are also quite numerous, but their reasoning is much sounder than that of those noted above. Most are based on the changes in vegetation and climate which had begun at the end of the Lower Cretaceous, and on the final split and isolation of the various continents. The actual spread of the flowering plants was unlikely to be the direct cause of extinction, for numerous ornithopod families had already adapted to feeding on them at an early stage in

Triceratops was represented in the uppermost Cretaceous by several distinct species. The form of the frill, and the size of the nose and brow horns being important identification features.

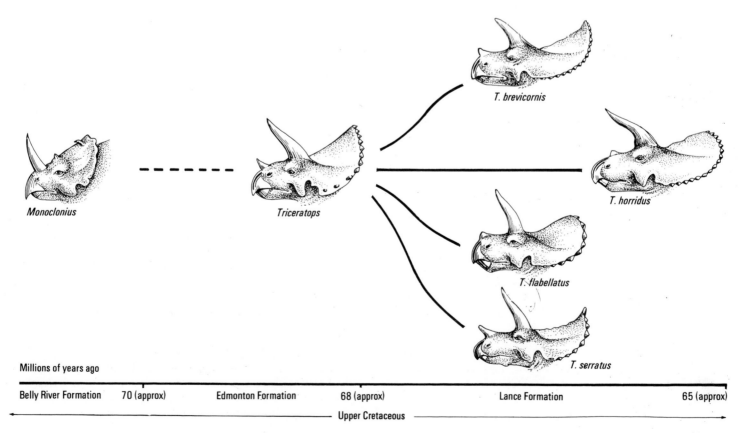

Millions of years ago

| Belly River Formation | 70 (approx) | Edmonton Formation | 68 (approx) | Lance Formation | 65 (approx) |

Upper Cretaceous

their development. Chemical changes within the flowering plants could be more critical, however; the build up of tanins and the appearance of new floras containing a high percentage of alkaloids making many plants unpalatable to the dinosaurs. Alternatively the dinosaurs' taste buds could have been poorly developed and the unsuspecting animals could have died of accumulative food poisoning. The new plants could have also affected the production of hormones within the body, with the result that the dinosaurs laid infertile eggs.

Numerous thin-shelled eggs have been collected from Upper Cretaceous deposits of southern France, and scientists have claimed that this phenomenon was related to drought. The lack of calcium in the shell would have affected the development of the embryonic dinosaur and subsequently reduced its ability to reach the hatchling stage. Drought is hardly a viable reason for worldwide extinction, however, and if the phenomenon of thin-shelled eggs proved to be more widespread, it is possible that diet or climate would have been much more critical. In fact a microscopic study of the thin-shelled eggs has shown that the deposition of calcium was irregular and this evidence has been presented in support of the theory that the parent animal lived in an area of temperature fluctuation. This point would in itself be difficult to prove and would certainly not be acceptable to those scientists who believe that the dinosaurs were warm-blooded and less affected by temperature variation. Unlike turtles and crocodiles, the dinosaurs laid hard-shelled eggs and it is possible that Upper Cretaceous dinosaurs suffered a lack of calcium in their diet. This would account for the thin nature of the egg shells and may have finally resulted in dinosaurs becoming 'egg bound'. Events of this type are known to happen to birds, and if they were to continue for a long time throughout the world, they would have had a dramatic effect on the survival potential of the group.

Climatic changes related to the drifting of the continents were without doubt critical to the survival of the dinosaurs. By the end of the Cretaceous the various land masses had achieved their present day outlines, and seasonal climates and rather cooler conditions affected many regions. Winter seasons would have had a disastrous effect on the dinosaurs' metabolic rate, with the result that they suffered a drop in body temperature and were rendered unable to feed. The fossilized skins of dinosaurs such as *Anatosaurus* are scaly, and indicate that the animals lacked an effective means of insulation. Even warm-blooded dinosaurs would therefore have suffered in the climatic extremes of the various seasons. Many animals faced with adverse climatic conditions migrate, but the split of the continents and the building of great mountain chains made this impossible for the dinosaurs. Isolated, they would have been placed at the mercy of localized conditions and microclimatic changes, disease and droughts could have affected and eliminated many local populations. Climatic changes are also thought to have brought about an increase in the force of the world's winds and a general increase in air turbulance. This may have had no direct effect on the dinosaurs, but was instrumental in the extinction of the delicately structured pterosaurs. As the drifting of the continents was a comparatively slow affair, one would expect that the changes in climate would also be gradual. Many scientists agree with this and refer to the steady decline in the variety of dinosaurs during the Upper Cretaceous for support. Others, however, believe that the climatic changes were sudden and extremely severe due to the explosion of a supernova. This explosion of some distant star would have bombarded the earth with X-rays, causing great turbulence and a drastic drop in temperatures throughout the world. Radiation levels would also have risen and, together with the drop in temperature, could be used to explain the extinction of the larger terrestrial organisms. This supernova theory is attractive to catastrophists, but as no extensive graveyards mark the end of the dinosaurs we can only suggest that their extinction was a slow process; a losing battle against insurmountable odds.

The survival of reptiles such as the turtles, crocodiles, snakes and lizards is difficult to explain in the light of dinosaur extinction, but it is likely that many of them survived because they were able to withstand the variation in seasonal climates by hibernating, and because they belonged to a different food chain to the dinosaurs. Their sources of food may have been restricted to soft vegetation, insects and each other; they would have fed well during the hot seasons but would have hibernated throughout the difficult winter months. Unfortunately many dinosaurs were too large to hibernate and as their sources of food would be extremely limited during winter seasons, gaps would soon appear in their food chains. The plant eaters would be the first to die out, followed by the meat eaters for whom the surviving snakes, lizards or tiny mammals would have made a paltry meal.

The extinction of the dinosaurs enables palaeontologists to dwell on the unknown and to play with the pieces of an incomplete jigsaw puzzle. It remains one of the unsolved mysteries of our science, with most people opting for a combination of events to explain away the disappearance of a superior group of animals. Of course, the presence of the birds may be just another expression of the evolutionary capabilities of an ancient dinosaur stock, with birds being the modern-day representatives of the agile coelurosaurs.

The colour plates in this book were illustrated by the following artists:

Ann Baum; the plates on pages 57, 69, 81, 83, 85, 113, 115, 121

Mary Lacey; title spread depicting *Heterodontosaurus* (left foreground), some coelurosaurs (left background) and *Melanorosaurus*, and the plates on pages 43, 47, 49, 61, 89, 99, 101, 109, 117, 119

Thomas Crosby-Smith; the plates on pages 45, 97

Tony Morris; the plates on pages 53, 55, 63, 73, 87, 91, 103, 105, 107, 111

Michael Youens; the plates on pages 51, 59, 65, 67, 71, 75, 77, 79, 93, 95

The colour plates

The following colour plates depict some of the more unusual and interesting animals recorded from the Age of Dinosaurs. As well as dinosaurs and their contemporaries, there are also some reconstructions of animals important in the evolution of the group.

Euparkeria and

(Greek, true thecodont, W.K. Parker (scientist's name)

Cynognathus

(Greek, dog-jaw)

Euparkeria and *Cynognathus* lived over 215 million years ago in the Lower Triassic communities of South Africa. Both were carnivores and they were representative of two very important groups of reptiles.

Cynognathus was a mammal-like reptile, the structure of its body representing an important step in the evolution towards the Mammalia. It was typically quadrupedal with short legs. The head was comparatively large and somewhat dog-like, and the teeth were differentiated into incisors, canines and cheek teeth. These last were cusped, the whole dentition being suited for seizing, tearing and chewing flesh. *Cynognathus* grew to about 2 metres (6·5 feet) in length, with its lizard-like body ending in a fairly short but powerful tail. In recent reconstructions the animal has been covered in hair and made to look very dog-like. The evidence for this is limited, but fits in well with the idea that they were also warm-blooded. *Cynognathus* and its relatives were the ruling predators of their day, forcing the developing thecodontians to adopt new pastures.

Among the early archosaurs was the form *Euparkeria,* a bipedal predator. It was less than half the size of *Cynognathus* and probably much more agile. Unlike the mammal-like reptile, however, the skull of *Euparkeria* was more lizard-like, and the teeth were less differentiated. They were strong and pointed, their essential role being to pierce the flesh of unwary prey. *Euparkeria* is recognized as the first reptile to walk erect, and its back legs were larger than the front legs. The legs were drawn close to the body, and when running the animal would arch its body with the head and tail lifted high off the ground. The lightly built body and bipedal nature of *Euparkeria* were essential to its success, enabling it to avoid the vicious teeth of its mammal-like contemporaries.

Cynognathus and the other mammal-like reptiles were content to evolve slowly within the lowland environments. The archosaurs were forced to experiment and by the Middle Triassic had become the dominant reptile group. *Euparkeria* was an early thecodontian and is often presented as the ancestral form from which all later archosaurs arose. Included among these were the dinosaur stocks which were to rule the world for over 140 million years.

Mandasuchus

(Manda, Tanzania, and Greek, crocodile)

Earlier in this book we followed the rise of the archosaur reptiles until they either dominated or replaced most other forms. The early archosaurs were called thecodontians, and it was from them that the dinosaurs, pterosaurs, crocodiles and birds evolved. The thecodontians themselves were divided into several groups, of which the pseudosuchians are the most important.

Mandasuchus is a typical pseudosuchian the remains of which, as the name suggests, have been found in the Manda Formation of Tanzania, Africa. *Suchus* in Greek means crocodile and in some ways *Mandasuchus* could be described as crocodilian. It was quadrupedal, spending all of its life on all four legs, unlike its earlier relative *Euparkeria* which was the first animal to walk in an upright or erect position. *Mandasuchus'* legs were drawn closer to the body, and it must have resembled a fast-moving crocodile – especially as it grew to crocodilian size. It was a carnivore with large teeth, and it would appear that the animal itself was not only larger, but also more efficient than many of its mammal-like reptile rivals. *Mandasuchus* lived over 200 million years ago in the Middle Triassic. The area in which it lived also supported plant eaters such as the dicynodonts and the rhynchosaurs. *Mandasuchus* must have hunted these and other creatures, and may have taken to killing small or injured meat eaters. Unlike the crocodiles, *Mandasuchus* spent most of its life on dry land, although it is unlikely that it would have wandered far away from the more humid lowlands. When running, *Mandasuchus* would have appeared to dip forwards, for the hind legs were slightly longer than the front ones.

After a kill the animal would tear at the carcass and, having torn off great chunks, would bolt them down very quickly. It is possible that like its close relative *Ticinosuchus* from the Monte San Giorgio area of Switzerland, *Mandasuchus* hunted and scavenged along the edge of lakes or even the seashore. Around the lakes the flora would have been dominated by horsetails whilst seed ferns flourished in drier areas. The deposits of Monte San Giorgio were laid down in the sea whereas those of the Manda Formation represent terrestrial environments. It is this variation that leads us to believe that quadrupedal pseudosuchians may have hunted their prey over quite an area. In the upland regions the first dinosaurs would have begun to establish themselves as a small, but significant, component of this East African community.

Ornithosuchus

(Greek, bird crocodile)

During the Upper Triassic Period, thecodontians and dinosaurs existed in various communities throughout the world. Normally it is possible to identify the fossil remains of these reptiles and refer them to their respective families. Occasionally, however, a specimen is discovered which shares characters of the two groups and it becomes difficult to decide to which it belongs. To rely on one set of characters, for example, might make it an advanced thecodontian, whilst choosing the others would infer that it is a primitive dinosaur. *Ornithosuchus* is such an animal, and in recent years it has been described under both headings. Its remains were discovered in the Upper Triassic sediments of Scotland and, when reconstructed, indicated that it was an agile biped.

The skull and lower jaw were lightly built, and the presence of numerous sharp, dagger-like teeth betray its feeding habits. *Ornithosuchus* reached 3 metres (10 feet) in length and stood at just over 1 metre (3·3 feet). The body was also slightly built, and well balanced on limbs drawn very close to its trunk. This means that the legs moved backwards and forwards in a line, a considerable improvement over the sprawling gait of many earlier archosaurs. *Ornithosuchus* was, therefore, able to run very quickly and to dodge and weave with considerable dexterity. Not surprisingly the feet of *Ornithosuchus* were adapted to this mode of life; the middle three toes being elongate and rather bird-like. When it ran, *Ornithosuchus* moved on its toes, the head and tail acting as counterbalances. The fore limbs were small, with five fingers which were probably used to hold food. *Ornithosuchus* lived at the same time as the small coelurosaur dinosaurs, and to some extent they filled the same ecological niche. Both were carnivores and it is likely that they fed on small reptiles or scavenged larger carcasses. If *Ornithosuchus* was an advanced thecodontian, it may well have existed in an area where the coelurosaurs were missing and would therefore reflect the ability of its group to adapt and occupy a vacant niche. In time, when the dinosaurs invaded its territory, *Ornithosuchus* would have lacked the ability to compete.

Thecodontosaurus

(Greek, socket-toothed lizard)

Thecodontosaurus was a prosauropod dinosaur, the remains of which have been recorded in several regions of the world in sediments of the Middle and Upper Triassic. As a prosauropod, the animal represented a probable link between the thecodontians and the great sauropods of the Jurassic and Cretaceous Periods. Most prosauropods were capable of both quadrupedal and bipedal movement and *Thecodontosaurus* was no exception to this rule. It spent most of its life on all four legs, but to reach food or to avoid attack it may have resorted to using its back legs only.

In many ways the animal was a mixture of primitive and advanced characters. It attained a length of some 3 metres (10 feet); the neck and tail accounting for the majority of this measurement. The head was relatively small, and the teeth were serrated. Whilst the front teeth resembled the simple cones of the thecodontians, the cheek teeth were broad and flattened, like those of herbivores. *Thecodontosaurus* had a much longer neck than its thecodontian ancestors and this may also represent an adaptation towards a plant-eating mode of life. These structural changes were incomplete, however, and the animal probably had a varied diet of flesh and plant materials. Its limbs were rather slender compared with those of later forms such as *Plateosaurus*. The hands and feet had rather long fingers and toes, and the back legs were longer than the front ones. *Thecodontosaurus* had a rather bulky body and a long tail, and would appear at first sight to have been easy prey for an active carnivore.

A wide geographical distribution and its presence throughout the latter half of the Triassic Period, however, suggest that it was a very successful animal. *Thecodontosaurus* must have occupied a niche beyond the domain of the voracious thecodontians, feeding on plants or the carcasses of animals. It may have also functioned as a predator searching for smaller, slower-moving reptiles. *Thecodontosaurus* had no obvious advantages over any of its contemporaries, yet was able to survive where they could not. In recent articles the prosauropods have been closely linked with the origin of the 'bird-hipped' dinosaurs. But, as the earliest ornithischian appears to occur before many prosauropods, it would be safer at this stage to regard *Thecodontosaurus* and its relatives as the base of sauropod evolution. Some of their descendants were to show a 40-fold increase in size and reached a body weight of over 100 tonnes.

Coelophysis and a phytosaur

(Greek, hollow form)

The scene opposite indicates that animals such as *Coelophysis* and the phytosaurs lived at the same time, and probably in the same region. The phytosaurs were aquatic, however, and represented a specialized branch of the early archosaurs. They were abundant during the late Triassic and many of them reached gigantic proportions. *Rutiodon* was a typical phytosaur; it was quadrupedal, and its body was covered in a heavy armour. The head was characterized by the long snout, and the positioning of the nostrils between the eyes. Phytosaurs occupied the same niche as the modern-day crocodiles, spending most of their day basking on raised mounds within their swampland home. They were meat eaters, feeding on fish and the occasional reptile or amphibian that wandered too close.

Coelophysis, an early theropod dinosaur of the coelurosaurian type, was unlikely to have been a victim of the phytosaurs. It was small and bipedal, with strong hind legs. *Coelophysis* probably inhabited the drier, more upland areas, and contact with the phytosaurs would have been rare. It was a carnivore, the long, pointed head being armed with numerous small, serrated teeth. The neck was very long and suggests that the head could be moved quickly in the search and capture of food. *Coelophysis* had small fore limbs, and the hands, with two long middle fingers and two shorter outer ones, were capable of grasping. The body was lightly built but the tail was more than half the length of the whole animal. Adults weighed a little over 20 kilograms (44 pounds) and reached 3 metres (10 feet) in length. The hind legs, although strong, were slender and the feet were bird-like. *Coelophysis* was an early 'lizard-hipped' dinosaur, and was an ancestor of both the later 'ostrich dinosaurs' and the birds. It was obviously a very agile creature capable of moving quickly, either in search of food or away from danger.

As we have seen earlier, large numbers of these animals existed in North America during the Upper Triassic. In times when food was short it could be that *Coelophysis* became cannibalistic. Mostly it fed on small prey, with reptiles or even primitive mammals forming the main part of its diet. The speed and agility of *Coelophysis* were its protection, and it is unlikely that this small creature had any armour over its body. Like its contemporaries in other parts of the world, and their Jurassic and Cretaceous descendants, *Coelophysis* was built for a particular role which it filled successfully.

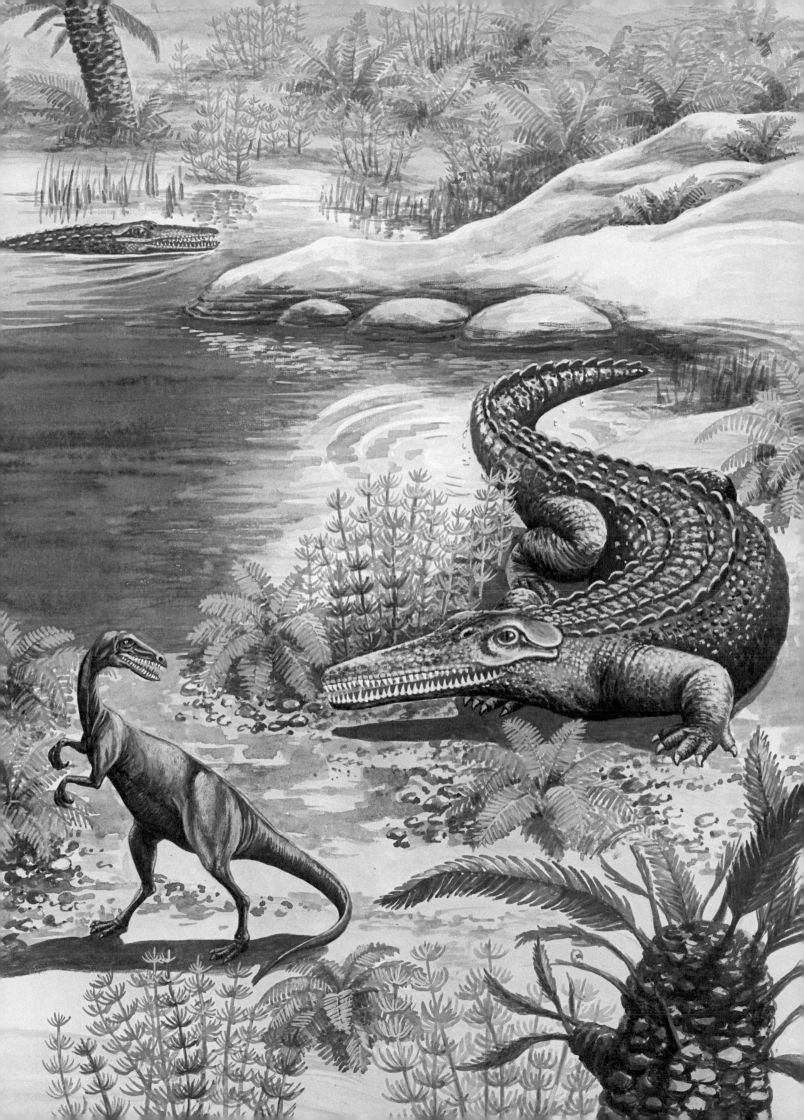

Fabrosaurus

(Fabre (Scientist's name), and Greek, lizard)

The remains of *Fabrosaurus* were first discovered in 1964 from the Upper Triassic sediments of Lesotho, South Africa. It is one of the limited number of ornithischian dinosaurs so far discovered in deposits of the Triassic Period. *Fabrosaurus* was a bipedal ornithopod which grew to approximately 1 metre (3 feet) in length. The head was small, and numerous sharp teeth lined the jaws. Anteriorly the jaws were rather beak-like, and the front of the lower jaw was most likely covered with a horny sheath – this is a characteristic feature of many ornithischins, and is a clue to the plant-eating habits of the group. Like most bipeds, *Fabrosaurus* had fore limbs which were much shorter than the hind limbs. This difference is an indication not only of an erect posture but also of an animal built for speed.

Fabrosaurus lived in the safe upland areas, for in the lowlands numerous thecodontians and other carnivores searched for food. In seeking the protection of the upland areas, *Fabrosaurus* exposed itself to the rigours of a more arid climate and would have probably encountered many problems in the control of its body temperature. In our illustration one animal is seen to be sheltering from the heat of the day. As with other small animals, *Fabrosaurus* would have had more problems than, say, the larger melanorosaurids, which inhabited the lowland regions of the same area in slightly earlier times. The melanorosaurids, although protected by a more humid climate, would have taken days to warm up or cool down, for they had a smaller surface-area-to-volume ratio. *Fabrosaurus*, on the other hand, would have exposed a greater surface area relative to its total weight, and would have either gained or lost heat quickly. If *Fabrosaurus*, like modern day reptiles, was ectothermic (dependent on the heat of the sun to warm its own body) then it probably spent much of the day and night in an inactive state. But even if it was endothermic (warm-blooded) it would have probably sought shelter from the heat of the midday sun.

Apart from the thecodontians, prosauropod and possibly sauropod dinosaurs lived in the lowland regions. In the main they were quadrupedal creatures depending on their great size for protection. *Fabrosaurus* was, as already mentioned, capable of great speed, and it was probable that this was also a defence mechanism, although its actual enemies are unknown.

Plateosaurus

(Greek, flat lizard)

Plateosaurus was a saurischian, or 'lizard-hipped', dinosaur that lived 200 million years ago; its remains having been collected from the Upper Triassic deposits of Germany. It was a large animal for its time, being 6 metres (19·5 feet) or more in length. Together with *Melanorosaurus* from South Africa and *Lufengo-saurus* from China, *Plateosaurus* represented a significant increase in size over its thecodontian ancestors. It was a plant eater which lived in and around the lowland swamps. The body was very bulky – a common characteristic of animals that consumed large quantities of plant material. In many ways *Plateosaurus* closely resembled the great sauropods of the Jurassic and Cretaceous Periods. The skull was quite small and the teeth flat and somewhat leaf-shaped. Both the neck and tail were long, the heavy tail accounting for almost half of the body length. The fore limbs of *Plateosaurus* were smaller than the hind limbs, but they were stoutly built, and the structure of the hands suggests that they could support part of the animal's weight. *Plateosaurus* spent much of its life on all fours but, during feeding or running, was capable of adopting a two-legged posture. The hind feet were broad, but unlike *Melanorosaurus* the toes were elongate with strong claws. In *Melanorosaurus* the feet were club-like, more like those of the gigantic sauropods.

Plateosaurus shared its lowland environment with the meat-eating theropods, the heavily built rhynchosaurs and numerous amphibians. Among the amphibians, *Mastodonsaurus* was by far the largest, its skull alone measuring over 1 metre (3 feet) in length. Whilst the plateosaurs roamed in herds, the small coelurosaurs hunted individually, searching for their next prey among all the different animal stocks. *Plateosaurus*, because of its ability to reach up on its hind limbs, was able to feed on both high and low-level vegetation. The food it sought was soft and easy to cut and grind, whilst the food of the powerfully jawed rhynchosaurs consisted of the tough seeds and roots of the seed ferns. In the Triassic swamps of the German lowlands the first turtles also appeared, their heavy, box-like shell protecting them against all but the most determined foe.

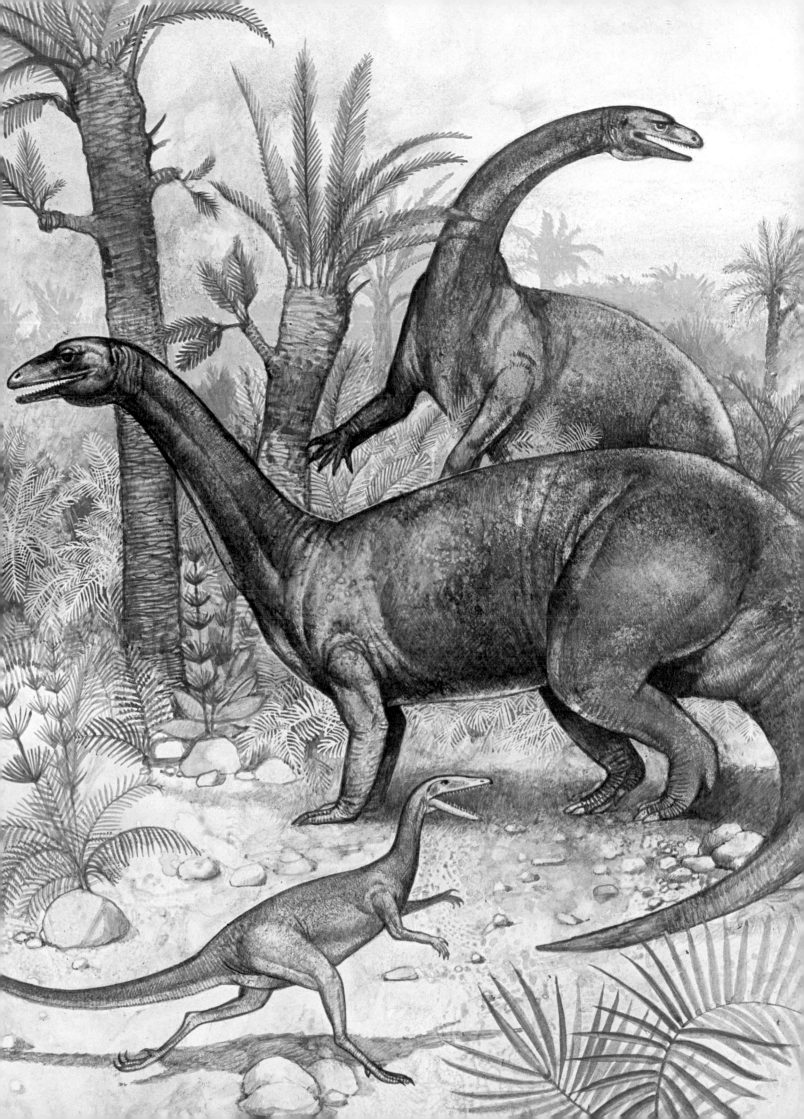

Megalosaurus

(Greek, big lizard)

Like *Allosaurus* and *Tyrannosaurus,* the 'big lizard' was a carnosaur. It was typically bipedal, the back legs being several times larger than the arms. The head was enormous, and the jaws were lined with rows of large, sharp teeth. *Megalosaurus* stood over 4 metres (13 feet) high and was 6 to 7 metres (19·5 to 23 feet) in length. Smaller and somewhat less bulky than *Tyrannosaurus,* it weighed around 2·5 tonnes.

During the Jurassic and Lower Cretaceous, *Megalosaurus* existed alongside a large and varied population of herbivorous dinosaurs. Among these were the great sauropods such as *Cetiosaurus* and *Apatosaurus,* and iguanodonts like *Camptosaurus* and *Iguanodon.* These were gigantic creatures, but the structure and agility of *Megalosaurus* would make them likely prey. During the chase, *Megalosaurus* would sprint along with its tail held up off the ground. Its body would tend to sway from side to side and, from trailways found in many areas, we see that the feet would land one almost directly behind the other, the footprints indicating a slight turn inwards of the clawed feet. As with other carnosaurs the foot had three large toes. These were clawed like those of a bird of prey and would without doubt be used in the attack of a selected victim. A blow with its back leg or a savage bite on the victim's back would give *Megalosaurus* the chance to slow the herbivore down. To kill, it would need to savage its prey or strike continuously at the neck and trunk area. *Megalosaurus* would then consume part of the victim, tearing great chunks of flesh from the carcass with its huge jaws. Trapped or injured animals would stand no chance against the onslaught. According to the geological record, animals referred to the genus *Megalosaurus,* existed for over 90 million years. If this is true then they represent one of the most successful vertebrate animals ever known, for whilst so many exotic creatures evolved around them, the megalosaurs remained almost unchanged. Change is really adaptation, which equips an animal with the ability to meet the challenge of environmental conditions. To remain unchanged suggests that *Megalosaurus* had found an almost perfect niche for itself. Its mode of life was well suited to its environment, and as a giant carnivore it preyed upon an abundant supply of plant eaters. The illustration here shows *Megalosaurus* about to attack a trapped *Iguanodon.*

Megalosaurus was the first dinosaur to be described, and if one accepts the subsequent identification of the bone figured as 'Scrotum humanum', as a femur of this giant carnosaur, then *Megalosaurus* was also the first dinosaur to be discovered by Man.

Scelidosaurus

(Greek, limb lizard)

The 'limb lizard' roamed the world 185 million years ago. It was an ornithischian dinosaur which for many years was considered to be the first of the 'bird-hipped' dinosaur line. *Scelidosaurus* was a heavily built creature, adult forms growing to just over 4 metres (13 feet) in length. The head was small compared with the bulky trunk, and the limbs were spread outwards, to support its large weight. *Scelidosaurus* walked slowly on all fours.

Like all ornithischians the 'limb lizard' was a plant eater. The size of the skull, together with the presence of rather weak jaws and unspecialized teeth, indicate that it fed on soft vegetation. The hind limbs were longer than the front ones and the animal probably grazed in a head-down position, the relatively long neck enabling it to reach the vegetation underfoot. Unlike those of the later ankylosaurs and stegosaurs, the feet of *Scelidosaurus* were rather unspecialized and non hoof-like.

As with all plant eaters, *Scelidosaurus* would eventually have come face to face with a flesh-eating dinosaur. Unfortunately its array of defence mechanisms was limited, speed and size being denied it. The jaws and teeth would have been useless against a creature such as *Megalosaurus*, and it is more than likely that *Scelidosaurus* would have tried to hide. If this was impossible the last line of protection was the rows of armour plates in the skin. Initially these may have deterred the predator from making the attack, the scelidosaur appearing more formidable than it actually was. Rows of plates ran from the back of the head to the tip of the tail. Ten or twelve rows existed over the area of the trunk, the top rows being slightly larger than those on the sides. The plates on the tail were organized in a similar way, although the plates of the top and bottom rows were the largest of all. In battle *Scelidosaurus* may have lashed with its tail in the hope of driving its tormentor away. If spared, it may have sought refuge in the dense vegetation near the seashore or river's edge, somewhere where the carnosaurs would find movement difficult.

Scelidosaurus was a short-lived genus, but from it rose the abundant and well-protected stegosaurs and ankylosaurs of the Jurassic and Cretaceous Periods. It is also important in that it was the first ornithischian to be described. The description, of an isolated specimen from the Lower Jurassic shales of Dorset, England, was presented by Sir Richard Owen in 1861. Marine invertebrates are among the most common fossils found in the shales and it is likely that the carcass of the 'limb lizard' was transported out to sea after death.

Apatosaurus

(Greek, deceptive lizard)

Until recently the remains of this great sauropod were described under two names – *Apatosaurus* and *Brontosaurus*. The last name was probably the best known, but unfortunately it is the more recent of the two, and therefore palaeontologists must use *Apatosaurus* in the description of any remains. Unlike *Brachiosaurus,* the 'deceptive lizard' had fore limbs which were shorter than the hind limbs. This resulted in the body of the animal sloping downwards towards the neck. This huge animal attained a length of over 22 metres (72 feet) and weighed approximately 30 tonnes. It was much heavier than its close relative, *Diplodocus,* even though it was some 5 metres (16·5 feet) shorter. The reason for the difference in weight between the two animals was that *Apatosaurus* had larger, heavier limb bones, and was generally more bulky. It had a comparatively large head and a thick, elongate neck. The backbone was made up of numerous large vertebrae which, unlike the bones of the limbs and girdles, were hollowed out. Vertical spines provided centres for muscle attachment over the back and along part of the tail, and lifting the neck resembled the raising of a crane jib in a dockyard. The brain of *Apatosaurus* earned no superlatives for it was even smaller than those of its two sauropod relatives, and would tend to support the theory of a slow-moving, rather unintelligent creature. No evidence exists for the so-called 'second brain' of *Apatosaurus,* although nerve centres several times the size of the true brain existed in the hip region. The functions of the brain were probably limited to the co-ordination of reflexes and the receipt of external stimuli.

Apatosaurus and its relatives have been described as 'walking automatons', a view which greatly contradicts the ideas of some recent researchers. This recent work, based on a comparison of the sauropods with the elephants, removes the giant dinosaurs from their aquatic environment and suggests that like the great mammals they were plain and forest dwellers. In this niche *Apatosaurus* apparently used its long neck to browse off tall vegetation, sometimes rising on to its hind legs to gain height and reach the highest leaves. Unfortunately, experiments carried out on sauropod tracks – left incidentally in mud at the edge of lakes – indicate that *Apatosaurus* could only move at between 3 and 6 kilometres (2 and 4 miles) per hour. At this speed they would surely have been at the mercy of the fleet-footed, land-dwelling carnosaurs.

Brachiosaurus

(Greek, arm lizard)

Brachiosaurus, the 'arm lizard', was the largest animal ever to have lived on land. It was a giant sauropod known from both North America and East Africa, from Upper Jurassic deposits of 150 million years ago. Compared with *Diplodocus* it was slightly shorter, but in bulk and height, it had no peer. *Brachiosaurus* was over 26 metres (85 feet) long and weighed 75 tonnes. The body was very stout and because the front legs were longer than the back ones, the back sloped down towards the tail. Longer front legs were the exception rather than the rule among dinosaurs, and in this respect, *Brachiosaurus* and its atlantosaurian relatives could be regarded as exceptional forms. In recent times the discovery of thigh bones almost 3 metres (10 feet) in length has indicated that the head of *Brachiosaurus* was over 13 metres (42·5 feet) above the ground. Strangely the head was small and the brain was of almost ridiculous proportions for an animal of this size. Like other sauropods, *Brachiosaurus* must have been rather slow to respond to any external stimulus and its huge bulk was really its only protection.

The classic view of *Brachiosaurus* was of a giant, slow-moving creature living almost totally submerged in water. Structurally, the skeleton would appear to confirm this view, for whilst the limb bones were really heavy, the vertebrae of the backbone and neck were extremely light, yet very strong. The weight of the lower half of the body, in this case, would serve to hold the animal on the river bottom, whilst the long neck and the position of the nostril on the very top of the skull would allow it to live in water up to 12 or 13 metres (39 to 42·5 feet) in depth. Unfortunately, this view ignores the fact that at this depth the animal would be unable to breathe, due to the pressure of water on the chest and lungs. *Brachiosaurus* did not live with only its nostrils above water, neither did it run at 32 kilometres per hour (20 miles per hour) on land as is thought by some. It probably spent most of its life wading in lake-land areas, its body submerged to shoulder height. The head could then be either held high to browse off bank or shoreline vegetation, or low over the lake surface to feed on water-dwelling plants. To lay eggs, *Brachiosaurus* would leave the water and walk across the mudflats, in doing so it would leave behind great footprints. From the measurements that have been taken between prints, it has been estimated that the animal walked at 3 kilometres per hour (2 miles per hour).

Allosaurus

(Greek, strange lizard)

The 'strange lizard' lived during the Upper Jurassic. It was a giant carnosaur, well equipped to act as the major predator of that period. The adults grew to an incredible 11 metres (36 feet) in length and weighed approximately 5 tonnes. Numerous large herbivores roamed the swamplands and plains of North America during the Upper Jurassic, and *Allosaurus* may have ranged through a number of areas in its search for food. Typically bipedal, *Allosaurus* would have chased its victim at speed, the great clawed feet turning inwards to give the animal better balance. Having cornered its prey the carnosaur would launch into attack with claws and teeth, ripping and slashing. Few, if any, of the contemporary herbivores could have withstood such an attack and some, like the giant sauropods, would have been easy prey outside their swampland niche. *Allosaurus* may even have used its short but powerful arms during a kill, for they, too, were equipped with three large claws. After the combat, the great jaws would tear at the carcass and huge chunks of flesh would be bolted down. The structure of the skull and the jaws was such that the mouth could open enormously wide. Armed with teeth 8–10 centimetres (3–4 inches) long, *Allosaurus* was an incredible foe.

After it had fed, the carnosaur would probably have rested some little way from the carcass. Its great body would lay on the ground with the hind legs pulled beneath the trunk. Whilst it slept the carcass became a feeding ground for other creatures such as small coelurosaurs or a flock of pterosaurs. Carnosaurs such as the smaller *Ceratosaurus* may have also scavenged, causing the flying reptiles and coelurosaurs to flee in terror. When *Allosaurus* decided to feed again, it would straighten its legs, pushing the weight of the body on to the arms. A backwards lift of the head would then coincide with a thrust from the legs and the animal would be ready to walk. Often it returned to the same carcass to scavenge remaining flesh.

In ecological terms, *Allosaurus* would hardly be recognized as a herd animal, for if it was, the numbers of herbivores would have been swiftly depleted. Usually the 'strange lizard' is seen as a lone hunter, but it would be safe to suggest that it could have lived and fed in small family groups. It could be that the mother alone protected her young and killed to provide them with food.

Stegosaurus

(Greek, roof lizard)

Stegosaurus lived over 140 million years ago in the Upper Jurassic environments of western North America. It was a herbivorous ornithischian quadruped, whose head was very small compared with the body, and whose brain weighed 1/250th of the animal's total weight. In side view, *Stegosaurus* was characterized by the presence of the rather elongate head and the rise of its body up to the pelvic region. This rise was due to the differing lengths of the front and back legs, but was emphasized by the presence of a series of large, vertical plates. These occurred in slightly offset rows with the largest plates sited over the pelvis. In some reconstructions these plates have been placed flat over the back of the animal to serve as a protective armour. There is, however, no evidence for this, and it is more likely that the vertical plates served a dual function; one to give an impression of greater size and the other to act as cooling vanes. Recent research has shown that large spaces were present at the base of the plates and within the plates themselves. This suggests the presence of large blood chambers and that through the plates the animal could regulate the temperature of its body. The configuration of the plates is such that the animal obtained the maximum benefit from their presence.

Like other 'plated dinosaurs', *Stegosaurus* had a limited number of small teeth; the anterior portion of the jaws was beak-like and was probably covered by a horny sheath similar to that of recent turtles. It was, therefore, unable to crush and grind tough plants and would have fed on soft vegetation. *Stegosaurus* probably lived in lowland areas bordering a tropical sea; lakes and swamplands would have covered much of the landscape, and ferns and horsetails would have provided a good food source. The animal would have roamed the edges of the swamps, feeding on ground vegetation, its overall size and bulk suggesting that it never adopted a bipedal stance or fed from the higher levels of vegetation. It roamed in small herds with adults of 9 metres (29·5 feet) in length and 1·8 tonnes in weight dominating the group. The tails of the stegosaurs were armed with four great spikes, and a blow from this weapon would have caused serious injury to any would-be attacker.

Kentrosaurus

(Greek, prickly lizard)

During the Upper Jurassic, dinosaur communities existed in several areas of the world. In many cases the environment in which these communities thrived were alike and, not surprisingly, similar animals occupied equivalent niches. The classic faunas of the Morrison Formation of North America and the Tendaguru beds of Tanzania, East Africa, are but two examples where such a correlation is possible, with dinosaurs such as the sauropods, ornithopods, coelurosaurs and stegosaurs common to both areas.

Of the stegosaurs, *Kentrosaurus* and *Stegosaurus* appear to have occupied the same niche, one in Africa and the other in North America. Both were quadrupedal ornithischians and each was characterized by a small head and a large, bulky frame. *Kentrosaurus* was the smaller of the two. It grew to 5 metres (16·5 feet) in length and weighed somewhere in the region of 1 tonne. The weight was a reflection of its plant-eating habits and of the visceral mass contained inside the great, bowed rib cage. The head was flattened and rather elongate, and the jaws and teeth were weakly developed. In general, stegosaurs lacked the batteries of teeth present in ornithopods such as the iguanodonts and hadrosaurs, and it follows that they ate softer plant material. *Kentrosaurus* had relatively short fore limbs and the head hung low over the ground. Behind the head, the neck and anterior trunk area were protected by two rows of small, vertical plates. Eight pairs of long spines covered the remaining area of the back and the tail. Their arrangement was somewhat irregular, with the longest pair placed over the pelvis. The general appearance of the animal would have created considerable doubt in the brain of a potential attacker. As the fore limbs were short and held in a slightly straddled position, the pelvis was also the tallest part of the animal; coupled with the presence of the long spines, the back region would be a difficult area for a predator to attack. In a fight to survive, *Kentrosaurus* would have presented its foe with a view of its spiny rear and attempted to deter it with blows from the barbed tail.

From the abundance of remains found at Tendaguru, and from the evidence of its feeding habits, *Kentrosaurus* is thought to have been a herd animal, roaming the lowland regions of the Upper Jurassic landscape in search of areas covered in soft, succulent vegetation. Whilst it fed, pterosaurs glided silently overhead, rising and falling with the prevailing air currents.

Camptosaurus

(Greek, bent lizard)

Camptosaurus, an ornithopod, lived during the Late Jurassic Period at a time when the majority of dinosaurs were of the 'lizard-hipped' variety. Animals such as *Apatosaurus* waded in the swamps whilst predators like *Allosaurus* searched the shoreline for an unsuspecting victim. *Camptosaurus* was quite small in comparison with these giants, for adult forms reached only 5 metres (16·5 feet) in length. Like *Apatosaurus* they were herbivores, but weighed only 3·5 tonnes against the 50 to 80 tonnes estimated for the giant sauropod. Camptosaurs roamed in large herds, spending most of their life in open areas beyond the swamps and forests. When searching for feeding grounds members of the herd, with the exception of a few old animals, walked on their back legs. These were quite massive and suggest that these animals could sustain a two-legged gait for some distance. The fore limbs were shorter than the legs but were stout enough to support the animal when it grazed. Some old, heavy camptosaurs may have reverted to a four-legged stance, and sought the shelter of the forest during the last days of their life. The hands of *Camptosaurus* had five fingers and were rather broad structures; the feet, with three main toes, were like those of later ornithopods.

The head of *Camptosaurus* was relatively small, having a long, rather flat silhouette. Anteriorly the jaws had the appearance of a beak, which may or may not have had a horny cover. When feeding, the beak would be used to cut through plant stems; the tongue would then bring the food into the mouth, and there, numerous teeth would crush the food before it was swallowed. As in many other herbivorous dinosaurs, the jaw mechanism of *Camptosaurus* was such that the teeth of the upper and lower jaws came together at the same time to break food into small fragments.

The natural enemies of *Camptosaurus* included the giant carnosaurs, *Allosaurus* and *Ceratosaurus*. Herding would have offered some protection to the inoffensive plant eaters, but now and again a sick or aged animal would have been killed for food. Plated stegosaurs shared the same area as the camptosaurs and it is likely that both groups lost young and eggs to the ever-present coelurosaurs.

The suggestion of herding among the camptosaurs is founded on the discovery of numerous specimens from the Morrison Formation of the western states of North America. Individual skeletons ranged between 0·7 and 5 metres (2·3 and 16·5 feet) in length and seem to represent all but the smallest animals within the growth range of the species.

Compsognathus and

(Greek, boastful jaw)

Archaeopteryx

(Greek, ancient feather)

The scene opposite is set in an Upper Jurassic forest in southern Germany. Cycads, gingkoes and conifers from the background vegetation, whilst the animals are *Compsognathus* (left) and *Archaeopteryx*. The forest grew along the shore line of a tropical sea, and jellyfish, brittle stars and king crabs abounded in the shallow waters. *Archaeopteryx* and *Compsognathus* were only two representatives of the large terrestrial fauna, but they serve to illustrate an important event in the history of our planet.

Compsognathus was very small, growing to only 60 cm (2 feet) in length. Physically, this carnivorous coelurosaur was very lightly built, with thin-walled bones. The hind limbs were very long, with the lower leg bones considerably longer than the thigh bones. This condition is found in animals that can run very quickly, and it follows that *Compsognathus* was a fast-moving predator. The head tapered sharply towards the snout, and the jaws were armed with numerous sharp, pointed teeth. *Compsognathus* had a large, flexible neck which was important in the search for food, whilst the hands, which had three functional fingers, would have been used to hold flesh close to the mouth. In its overall appearance the animal looked like a bird without feathers – in fact it closely resembled a naked *Archaeopteryx*.

The structural differences between the smallest dinosaur and the first bird, although obvious to a skilled palaeontologist, were comparatively low in number. *Archaeopteryx* had a tapered snout, sharp teeth, a long tail and legs similar to the small dinosaur, but it also had very long fore limbs and a modified pelvis. Being a bird, *Archaeopteryx* also had feathers, a feature which some workers have also associated with *Compsognathus*. From the five specimens known of the first bird, it is obvious that the feathers were well formed, and that long ones covered the edges of both tail and wings. Unlike modern birds, 'ancient feather' had three fingers at the end of each wing; these have often been interpreted as claws which would have helped it climb trees. This interpretation is somewhat suspect, and it is more probable that *Archaeopteryx* lived in forest glades where it used its wings to trap insects and avoid capture and death at the hands of *Compsognathus*. In our scene the first bird is therefore seen to exist, albeit perilously, alongside a representative of the group from which it developed.

Hypsilophodon

(Greek, high-ridge tooth)

Hypsilophodon, a bipedal ornithopod, lived in the area of the Isle of Wight, England, during Wealden times. It was a small dinosaur between 1 and 1·2 metres (3·3 and 3·9 feet) in length. It was strongly bipedal, with the back legs more than twice the length of the front legs. The head was small and the jaws beak-like. Apart from a few teeth in the front of the upper jaw, the jaws were also toothless. The neck was of moderate length whilst the tail accounted for more than half of the body length.

Early reconstructions of the animal's form and function placed it in a forest environment, living as a tree dweller. The reasons for this included large eyes, and feet that would allow it to grasp branches. *Hypsilophodon* was later likened to a tree kangaroo, but more recently was thought to have lived like *Iguanodon*. Even this reconstruction has been questioned, and the most up-to-date suggestion is that the animal was an extremely agile herbivore.

In some ways *Hypsilophodon* was primitive, having a five-fingered hand and a four-toed foot. Small bony plates protruded from the skin and appeared to represent the last vestiges of the armour found in ancestral forms. The loss of teeth, and the presence of bony tendons in the tail suggest, however, that some advances had taken place. Bony tendons act to stiffen the tail and help hold it off the ground. It follows that if this were the case, *Hypsilophodon* ran with its backbone held horizontally, with the tail again acting as a counterbalance to the head. The proportions of the length of the shin bones to that of the thigh bones are similar to those of a gazelle or ostrich, and suggest a fast-running animal. When running, *Hypsilophodon* rose on to its toes and appears to have been able to bound and weave about in a manner reminiscent of a kangaroo. To a herbivore this was invaluable, enabling it to outrun and out-manoeuvre the most agile predators. *Hypsilophodon* lived in the forest glades along the early Cretaceous coastline. It shared its environment with *Iguanodon;* the two feeding on fruit and soft vegetation. Both animals roamed in small herds, ever alert against an attack by either the giant carnosaur *Megalosaurus,* or the more agile and more numerous coelurosaurs.

Deinonychus

(Greek, terrible claw)

Deinonychus, the 'terrible claw', was discovered in 1964 in the Lower Cretaceous deposits of Montana. It was a bipedal dromaeosaurid, an advanced coelurosaur with a larger than normal head and an enormous clawed toe. The animal grew to approximately 3 metres (10 feet) in length and stood just under 2 metres (6·5 feet) in height. It was lightly built and obviously adapted to a fast-running, predatory way of life. The head is usually featured as that of a rather elegant beast, and the eyes, comparatively large, suggest a higher-than-average reptilian intelligence. Bodily the animal was quite streamlined, although the neck was of rather stout construction. The arms, approximately half the length of the back legs, each bore three rather powerful clawed fingers, which appear to be ideal for grasping or tearing. The back legs were slender, yet powerful. Each foot had three toes, two of which reached the ground and another which was shortened, yet armed with the enormous claw noted above. The claw itself was sickle-shaped and over 12 centimetres (5 inches) in length. *Deinonychus* was also noted for the form of its tail which was held high and rigid through its life. Rods of thin bone sheathed the vertebrae of the tail to give it this rigid character and *Deinonychus* a high degree of agility.

In life the beast would have strutted, delicately balanced by the counterweights of head and tail. In the search for food. *Deinonychus* would have reached considerable speeds and would have been able to outrun all of the small creatures it pursued. To kill, it would have used the back legs, kicking at its intended prey with alarming ferocity as the accompanying plate shows. At first the victim would be knocked down, temporarily stunned, and then *Deinonychus* would turn and deliver the final blows using the inner claw like a dagger. The tail would balance the animal whilst it fed, and the hands could grasp and pull at the carcass.

The agility and speed attributed to *Deinonychus* would indicate that the animal had a high metabolic rate. *Deinonychus* has been used as evidence in support of the theory that the dinosaurs were warm-blooded. Small dinosaurs experienced greater problems in controlling their body temperature than did giants such as the sauropods, and warm-bloodedness would be the answer to their problems. Whatever the truth may be, *Deinonychus*, the 'terrible claw', was probably the most fearsome creature of its period.

Iguanodon

(Iguana and Greek, tooth)

As one of the first two dinosaurs to be described, *Iguanodon* is known to all students of palaeontology. Found first in 1822, iguanodonts have since been discovered throughout the world, and in some areas in considerable numbers. *Iguanodon* was a large bird-hipped ornithopod which lived during the Lower Cretaceous, 136–115 million years ago. It was a heavily built creature over 5 metres (16·5 feet) tall and 10 metres (33 feet) in length. Estimates of its weight vary but it was unlikely to be less than 5 tonnes. Descended from *Camptosaurus*, *Iguanodon* bore many of the characteristics of its ancestor. The head was obviously larger but still rather long and flat in profile. Unlike *Camptosaurus*, *Iguanodon* had several rows of teeth present along each jaw, with new teeth erupting continuously to replace those worn out during feeding. The arms were larger than those of its ornithischian ancestor, and the fore limbs of aged animals were proportionately larger than those of juveniles. No doubt this was to support an increase in body weight – it is a remarkable insight into the evolutionary capabilities of these beasts. *Iguanodon* used the batteries of teeth in its mouth to chop and crush plant material.

The area in which it lived was similar to the modern-day swamplands of Florida, with stretches of dry land raised just above the waterline. Primitive seed plants flourished in these dry regions, and it was on these that *Iguanodon* fed. Herds of animals roamed in search of food, picking fruits and leaves from several levels of vegetation. As an inoffensive herbivore, *Iguanodon* was likely prey for the giant carnosaurs. It would try at first to out-run its tormentor, but if trapped would attempt to drive the predator away with stabbing blows from its spike-like thumb. Blows from the tail and powerful legs may also have been used in defence.

It is possible that the herd of iguanodonts discovered in Belgium in 1878, fell to their death whilst being chased. Blind terror was just as likely to carry them over the edge of the ravine into which they supposedly fell, as were the flood waters postulated by many researchers. In fact, flood waters would have tended to scatter the skeletons far and wide and smash and shatter their bones. Whatever the correct answer, be it flood waters or the blind rush of a terrified herd into a ravine or glutinous swamp, the Belgian specimens rank among the greatest fossil discoveries in geological history.

Acanthopholis

(Greek, prickly scaled lizard)

During the Lower Cretaceous the stegosaurs, or plated dinosaurs, were succeeded by the armoured dinosaurs – the Ankylosauria. Early representatives of this group (including *Acanthopholis*) were but lightly armoured, lacking the extensive pavement
of bony plates and spines of their nodosaurian cousins. *Acanthopholis* grew to just over 3 metres (10 feet) long, the body being
comparatively narrow. The head was typically small but at the
same time flattened and elongate. The neck and shoulders were
covered in small spines whilst the body armour consisted of
numerous comparatively small plates. Although quadrupedal,
Acanthopholis had fairly short fore limbs and the body rose to
its maximum height above the pelvis. The tail was straight and
lacked the clubs and spikes of later more advanced species.

As with other reptiles, *Acanthopholis* laid eggs which were
protected by an outer shell. The eggs were laid in secluded
places and covered with sand or vegetation as camouflage from
the searching coelurosaurs. Before the female sought a suitable
nesting site the eggs were fertilized within her body. In fishes
or amphibians fertilization was usually external, taking place in
water, which both helped the process and protected the eggs
against desiccation. With the conquest of the terrestrial environment, however, the return to water would have been restrictive,
and to counter the problems of fertilization in arid conditions,
the male and female dinosaurs mated. The eggs were then
fertilized before the development of the shell and their deposition in the nest. It is possible that the female dinosaur remained
close to the nest until her young hatched out. Parental care of
nest and young is a fairly new concept, when related to the
dinosaurs, and is to some extent based on the discovery of
similar habits among the modern-day crocodiles. Young acanthopholids would have been easy prey for the agile coelurosaurs
or carnosaurs, and the presence of the parent could have been
important to the success and survival of both the individual and
the family.

The appearance of *Acanthopholis* and related ankylosaurs in
the Northern Hemisphere was part of the great expansion
among Cretaceous ornithopods; a wide variety of different types
of herbivores evolving in response to the climatic and floral
changes of the period. The evolution of the flowering plants
must have had a considerable effect on the herbivorous fauna of
the time, causing the extinction of some ancient stocks and
encouraging the evolution of new stocks to fill empty niches.

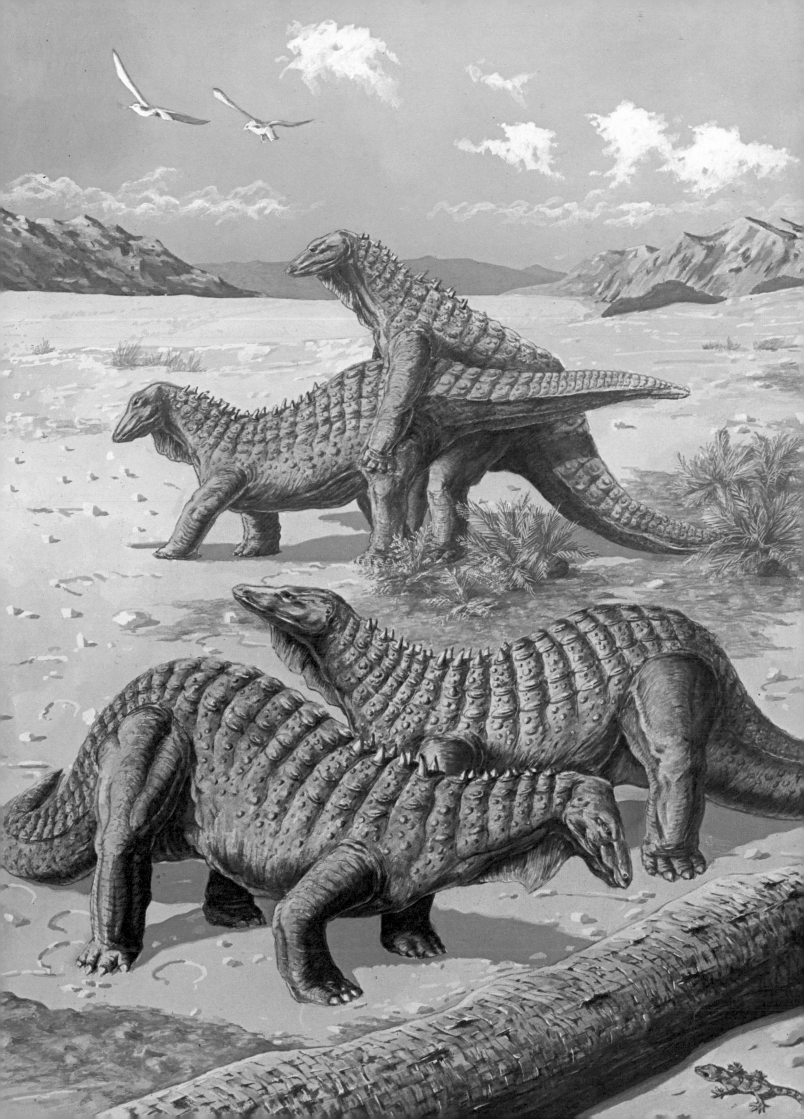

Polacanthus

(Greek, many spined)

Among the vast variety of ornithischians that evolved during the Cretaceous Period, one group, the ankylosaurs, developed a heavy, often spiny armour. *Polacanthus* was one of the early representatives of the group, living as it did in the Lower Cretaceous, over 120 million years ago. It was a rather squat animal which ambled around on all four limbs. The head of the creature is unknown, but we can assume that it was a relatively small structure. Two rows of spines stretch from the back of the head to an area just beyond the middle of the trunk. The largest spines occurred over the shoulders and the anterior region of the back, whilst the hips were protected by a large bony shield. A row of triangular plates ran along either side of the tail. *Polacanthus* was over 4 metres (13 feet) in length and weighed between one and two tonnes.

The huge spines and the bulky, rather flattened body, indicate that the animal was a slow, sluggish creature. It relied on its armour for protection when under attack, and in contrast to the more fleet-footed ornithopods, it could not outrun a bipedal carnosaur. If cornered, *Polacanthus* would have tried to push its way out of danger, the large spines proving painful to even the most persistent attacker. The back legs were much larger than the fore limbs, and with its head low, *Polacanthus* would prove a difficult adversary, because to deal a fatal blow the carnosaur would have to turn its prey either over or on to its side.

It is possible that because of its form and lack of agility, *Polacanthus* dwelt in the areas where the ground was soft under foot. Such conditions would deter fleet-footed predators and make the reptilian 'tanks' almost impossible to overturn. Support for this argument is found in the mouths of the ankylosaurs, for in the vast majority the teeth are small and weak, or even absent. This infers that they ate soft vegetation such as that found in the areas surrounding swamps or lakes. (Plants adapted to terrestrial conditions have thick cuticles and this type of food may have been unsuitable for these lumbering herbivores.) Whatever problems *Polacanthus* and its relatives faced, it is obvious that they were not insurmountable, as the group flourished throughout the Cretaceous Period. During the Upper Cretaceous ankylosaurs were found in large numbers in North and South America, Asia and Europe. *Polacanthus* itself is known only from the Lower Cretaceous deposits of the Isle of Wight, England.

Ouranosaurus

(Greek, heavenly lizard)

In recent years expeditions into the wastes of the Sahara Desert discovered the remains of the unusual Cretaceous ornithopod, *Ouranosaurus*. During its life time the area enjoyed a more agreeable climate; rivers crossed fertile plains and a rich growth of vegetation provided the animal with a source of food. When the animal died it was buried quickly, its skeleton remaining protected until exhumed by the harsh desert winds. Today, the skeletons of *Ouranosaurus* are found with their vertebral columns forming the crests of small sand dunes.

As an ornithopod, *Ouranosaurus* possessed a 'bird-hipped' pelvis and, like its close relative *Iguanodon,* it was essentially bipedal. It was approximately 5 metres (16·5 feet) tall, and the head was long and flat; the jaws were armed with numerous teeth. Behind the back of the head a series of blade-like processes arose from the vertebral column to give support to a sail. This ran over the back of the animal and along most of the tail. Its function was to stop *Ouranosaurus* overheating, for although the climate of the area where it lived was more equable than that of the recent Sahara, it was still hot. Like *Dimetrodon,* the mammal-like reptile with a sail back, and the carnosaur *Spinosaurus, Ouranosaurus* regulated its body temperature with the aid of its sail. In the cool of the morning the beast would turn its body sideways so that the sail was fully exposed to the warmth of the sun. This would serve to raise the body temperature and help the animal generate energy. When the body temperature was sufficiently high, *Ouranosaurus* would be able to move and feed easily. If the heat became too great, *Ouranosaurus* would then turn towards the sun; only the vertical line of the sail would now be exposed and heat would be lost along the length of the body.

It is probable that carnosaurs such as *Spinosaurus* existed in the same area as *Ouranosaurus*. If they did, then they would hunt it for food; without the sail *Ouranosaurus* would be easy prey for the sail-backed predator. Like *Iguanodon,* the ourano-saurs were probably gregarious, with many animals roaming together in search of food. The large numbers would have offered protection against the over-attentive carnosaur. The predator would stalk the herd at a distance, with the adult ouranosaurs of the herd keeping a watchful eye. In flight they would run using the power of their large hind legs; when resting they would adopt a squat position with some of the weight borne by the short, stout arms.

Spinosaurus

(Greek, spine lizard)

The Upper Cretaceous of Egypt has yielded the bones of a large sail-backed carnosaur named *Spinosaurus*. The presence of the unusual sail was established by the discovery of vertebrae with greatly elongated neural spines. Some spines measure as much as 2 metres (6·5 feet) in length, and the sail they supported extended from the middle of the neck to a point just behind the pelvis. The animal was over 11 metres (36 feet) long and, like its Jurassic ancestors, it had a large head, the jaws of which were lined with exceedingly sharp teeth. *Spinosaurus* was strongly bipedal although the fore limbs were quite robust with four strong fingers on each hand. The hind limbs were those of a typical carnosaur with three large toes making contact with the ground.

As a flesh eater *Spinosaurus* was probably quite active and would track its prey over open lands. The area where it lived was subject to a subtropical climate, and temperature control would have been quite a problem. On really hot days *Spinosaurus* would have used its sail to lose heat, turning its head directly towards the sun so giving the sides of the body a chance to cool down. In the mornings it would have exposed the side of its body to the sunlight and thus increased the body temperature to its normal level. Such control would give *Spinosaurus* a distinct advantage over many contemporary animals, in the same way as did the sail of the synapsid, *Dimetrodon*. However, evolution, like history, repeats itself and as in the case of the synapsids, herbivorous contemporaries of *Spinosaurus* also developed a sail. In their case the sail not only helped control their body temperature, it also restored the balance between them and the hunter. The sturdy front legs of *Spinosaurus* suggest that they played an important role in the life of the animal. They were proportionally larger than those of Jurassic relatives, and would indicate that the animal spent some time standing on all four legs. Much of this could have been linked with the control of the body temperature, the animal adopting a four-legged stance rather than resting in a vulnerable squat position. When hunting or tracking, *Spinosaurus* moved on its back legs. In terms of evolution the 'spiny' carnosaur appears to have been an adaptation to specific environmental conditions and is regarded as an interesting side branch of the carnosaur family tree.

Psittacosaurus

(Greek, parrot lizard)

In a classification of the dinosaurs, *Psittacosaurus* is placed among the ornithischians, and is generally regarded as a close relative of *Hypsilophodon*. Structurally, however, it shares some similarities with the horned dinosaurs and could represent the ancestral condition. Remains of *Psittacosaurus* have been found in China and Mongolia, in sediments deposited over 110 million years ago during the Lower Cretaceous. Geologically speaking this would be the right time for any ancestor of the Upper Cretaceous ceratopsians to appear.

The animal, like many other primitive ornithischians, was characterized by having long back legs. Presumably *Psittacosaurus* spent much of its life in a bipedal pose, although the sturdy nature of the fore limbs suggests that it may have also adopted a four-legged stance when feeding, as our illustration shows. Unlike the related *Hypsilophodon*, it was heavily built, and the head of the 'parrot lizard' was also different to those of the typical two-legged ornithischians. It was deep, and the snout narrowed into a sharp parrot-like beak. Only a limited number of teeth were present in the mouth, and the eyes and nostrils were placed high on the side of the head. These features, coupled with the presence of a very small, flat crest, link *Psittacosaurus* with the more specialized Upper Cretaceous ceratopsians. In some ways the animal bears more comparison to *Protoceratops*, the first true ceratopsian, than it does to the early bipedal stocks.

Psittacosaurus was a small animal about 2 metres (6·5 feet) in length, and its size and heavy build suggest that it spent most of its time grazing in forest glades. The neck was comparatively long and, as it could stand on its back legs, the animal was able to feed at several levels. Forest areas afforded the slow-moving *Psittacosaurus* the protective cover it needed to avoid the giant carnosaurs. In time the descendants of the 'parrot lizard' would develop their great frills and horns, and increase in size. The protection of the forest would then be unnecessary and great herds of horned dinosaurs would roam the open lands in relative safety. Ceratopsians were quadrupedal dinosaurs which cropped low vegetation; in the course of evolution they lost the grasping function of the hand which was a feature of their forest-dwelling ancestor.

Protoceratops

(Greek, first horned face)

Protoceratops was a 'bird-hipped dinosaur' which grew to 2 metres (6·5 feet) in length. Unlike its ancestor *Psittacosaurus*, it was completely quadrupedal, and spent its life cropping the vegetation of the Mongolian plains during the Upper Cretaceous. *Protoceratops* was the first of the horned dinosaurs – even though it lacked a horn! The head was deep and it narrowed anteriorly into a hooked, parrot-like beak. A large, bony frill covered the neck. In life the frill acted as an area of attachment for large jaw muscles and for the powerful neck muscles that supported the head, which was exceedingly large for such a small animal. *Protoceratops* lacked any body armour and would appear to have been rather vulnerable.

It existed in herds, and from the many skeletons discovered, appears to have prospered in spite of its vulnerability. Collections from the 'Flaming Cliffs' of Djadochta, Mongolia, include adults, juveniles and eggs, and present palaeontologists with an almost complete record of the growth of the animal. In the youngest hatchlings the frill is relatively short and flat. As growth continues, however, the frill appears to outpace the rest of the skull until in the adult it had attained enormous proportions. This 'irregular' development is difficult to explain, although it may have been related to the fact that if the young also had a large and heavy frill, they would have found it impossible to keep up with the herd.

The eggs found in association with the skeletons of *Protoceratops* were very important, for they proved that dinosaurs laid eggs and showed that the eggs were laid in nests. A female *Protoceratops* laid between ten and fifteen eggs which she subsequently covered with sand. She then returned to the herd to feed in close proximity to the nesting grounds. Parental instinct would make the female return to her nest on several occasions and it may be that, like the female crocodile, she helped her young into the world. From the evidence of a death struggle between a *Protoceratops* and the coelurosaur *Velociraptor*, it would appear that the horned dinosaur would have challenged any creature that attempted to destroy its progeny. Apart from *Velociraptor*, which would have fed on the young hatchlings, other fleet-footed dinosaurs such as *Oviraptor* would have raided the ceratopsian nests. Unable to match their agility the ceratopsian herd could have formed a protective screen around their nesting grounds.

Ornithomimus

(Greek, bird imitator)

Throughout the history of the dinosaurs one group, the coelurosaurs, were characterized by their light construction and two-
legged stance. They filled the roles of scavenger, insect eater
and killer of small animals. Various types thrived throughout
the world, the first ancestral forms appearing in the Middle
Triassic. With time the basic plan of the coelurosaurs changed
little, but the development of a horny beak, longer arms and
large eyes in certain individual types suggests that they were
becoming more and more specialized. *Ornithomimus* appeared
at a late stage in the history of the group and its structure indicates a particular mode of life.

Ornithomimus lived in the Upper Cretaceous between 120–
65 million years ago; it was a descendant of the early coelurosaurs such as *Coelophysis*. Unlike its ancestors, however, it had
toothless, beak-like jaws. The head was typically small and
very similar to that of an ostrich. This character was shared
with several other Cretaceous forms, and they are collectively
described as the 'ostrich dinosaurs'. *Ornithomimus* and its relatives were larger than their ancestors, the average length being
between 3·5 and 4 metres (11·5 and 13 feet). All were strongly
bipedal with long fore limbs. In the case of *Ornithomimus* the
lower leg bone was longer than the thigh bone, suggesting that
the animal was capable of running very quickly. The neck was
also elongate and flexible, allowing the head to be moved quickly
in a movement similar to the pecking motion of a chicken.
Ornithomimus had delicate, hollow bones, and when it ran the
head was carried in a fairly high position whilst the tail was held
horizontally.

The regions where the 'bird imitator' lived encompassed
several environmental areas ranging from coastal swamps and
lakes, through dense forests, to open lands. Speed was hardly
necessary in swamp or forest, and *Ornithomimus* is thought to
have lived, like the ostrich, in wide open spaces. Here it searched
for food; its diet included small lizards or mammals, insects and
fruit. It may also have eaten eggs, for herds of the early horned
dinosaur *Protoceratops* also inhabited the same area. In the
search for a nest, *Ornithomimus* may have used its hands, first to
clear the sand and then to pull the eggs into a position where
they could be cracked by a blow from the beak. The ornithomimids and other coelurosaurs probably survived until the end of
the Age of Dinosaurs because they were both omnivorous and
fleet of foot. It is unlikely that any other dinosaur could have
matched them for speed, and rather than await the attention of a
voracious tyrannosaur, they would have fled with long-legged
strides.

Saurornithoides

(Greek, bird-like reptile)

Like *Ornithomimus*, *Saurornithoides* was a two-legged dinosaur. It lived in the same region at the same time, but although 'bird-like', it is referred to a group called the dromaeosaurids. These were coelurosaurs with relatively large brain cases, and are thought by some palaeontologists to be among the most intelligent reptiles that ever lived. The group evolved from the genus *Dromaeosaurus*, the 'emu reptile', which lived in the earlier part of the Upper Cretaceous of Alberta, Canada.

The head of *Saurornithoides* was, by comparison, much larger than that of the 'bird imitator'. Sharp teeth lined the powerful, beak-like jaws and large eyes allowed good vision. The neck was long, but fairly robust. As with the ostrich-like dinosaurs, the fore limbs of *Saurornithoides* were elongate; the hands with long fingers were used for grasping. The powerful back legs again indicate a fleet-footed creature, the long, tapering tail acting as a counterbalance to the head. The feet were those of a theropod dinosaur with three main toes and a shortened inner toe.

Agility, excellent vision and a supposedly high degree of intelligence suggest that *Saurornithoides* was a rather special creature. Adult forms grew to about 2 metres (6·5 feet) in length, and it is probable that males, females and juveniles lived in family groups. Parents would have hunted food for their young, and the young in turn would have copied the adults and learned to search and kill. Improved vision may infer that these creatures hunted at night, feeding on nocturnal mammals. But it could also be an adaptation to an upland life, with *Saurornithoides* searching between rocks and in scrub for lizards and rat-like mammals. The grasping hands would be of considerable value in this type of environment, and could be used to shake the shrubs or pull at rocks. The feet would be used to pin the struggling prey to the ground. Pieces of flesh torn from the carcass could then be held in the hands whilst the animal tore off still smaller morsels.

Saurornithoides lived in close proximity to the plant-eating pachycephalosaurs which, according to some reports, existed in large herds in the upland areas of Mongolia during the latter part of the Upper Cretaceous. The pachycephalosaurs were defenceless apart from the thick, bony dome on the upper regions of the face and head. Adults would be too large for the 'bird-like' reptile to kill, but young hatchlings may have been a different proposition.

Velociraptor

(Greek, swift robber)

As its popular name suggests, the 'swift' or 'fast-running robber', was fleet of foot. *Velociraptor* was a bipedal saurischian, a lightly built predator from the Upper Cretaceous of Mongolia. It was a carnivorous coelurosaur and, according to recent work, is placed with dromaeosaurids (a group characterized by the presence of a large brain case and big eyes). *Velociraptor* ran on its strong hind limbs but, unlike earlier coelurosaurians, its fore limbs were relatively elongate. Its hands had three long fingers, the fourth and fifth fingers having been lost in the course of evolution. The wrist structure of *Velociraptor* was similar to that of *Deinonychus* and *Archaeopteryx*, and suggests a high degree of flexibility. The form of the hand and the mechanism of the wrist indicate that the whole fore limb played an important role in the life of the animal.

Velociraptor roamed across open lands searching for small reptiles or mammals. Frequently it would discover a nest, for herds of early horned dinosaurs lived in the same area. The robber may have broken the eggs and eaten the contents, but this form of food was difficult for it to consume, and was best left to its 'ostrich-like' relatives. In some cases, however, *Velociraptor* may have been drawn by sight or sound to a nest where the young protoceratopsians were emerging. The youngsters were defenceless and the agile predator would have had few problems in killing and eating them. A blow with the foot or head would be sufficient to kill the prey, which could then be lifted to the mouth by means of the grasping hands. The hands would then hold the flesh whilst the animal tore off and swallowed sizeable chunks.

Involved in devouring the hatchlings *Velociraptor* would not have noticed the approach of adult *Protoceratops*. Intent on protecting its young the frilled herbivore would have challenged the carnivore. A battle would have taken place with the agile *Velociraptor* attempting to lure *Protoceratops* away from the young. *Protoceratops* was extremely limited as a fighter and could only protect the nest by using its body as a shield. In some instances this may have worked, but in most it was likely that *Velociraptor* succeeded in its attempts. On one occasion, however, both animals lost; for in 1971 a joint Polish-Mongolian expedition found the remains of *Protoceratops* and *Oviraptor* locked together in a death struggle. The hands of the small theropod were seen to be gripping the frill of the herbivore, but the actual cause of death of both creatures is unknown.

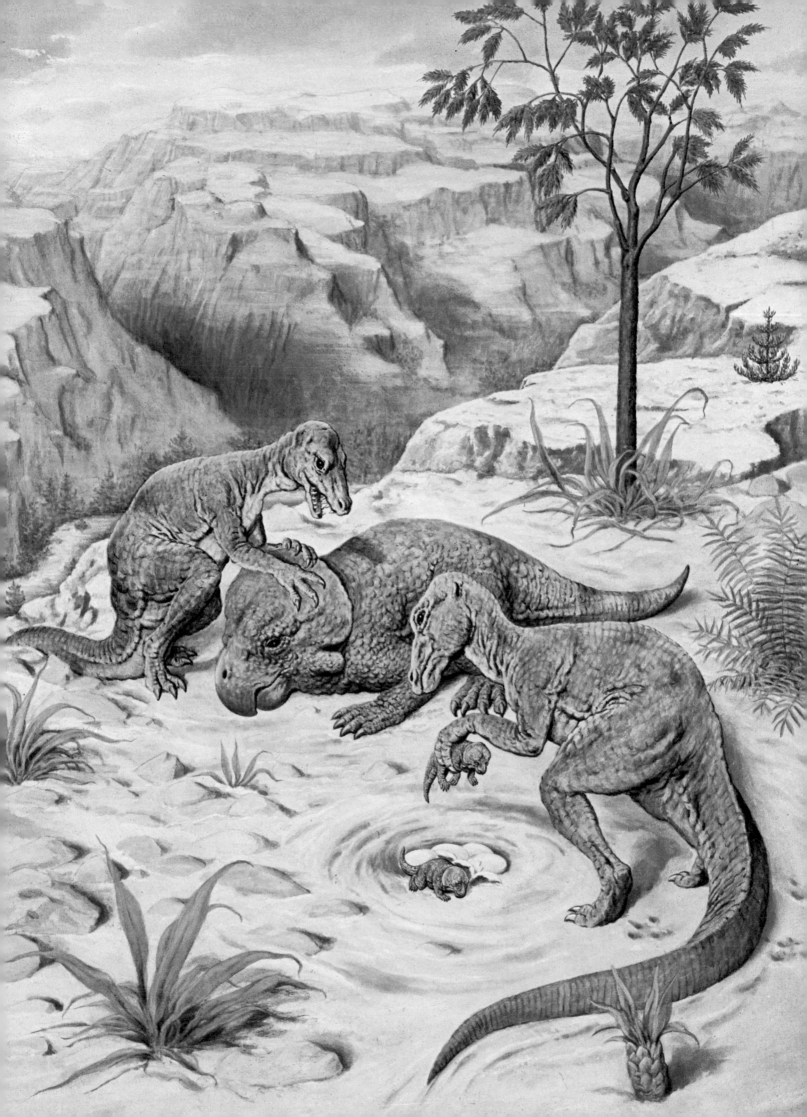

Leptoceratops

(Greek, slender-horned lizard)

In a general account of the evolution of the horned dinosaurs, or ceratopsians, one would see a general increase in the size of the body, and an elaboration of the frill and horns. The protoceratopsians would therefore represent the base of the trend and the huge *Triceratops* or *Torosaurus* the peak. Most intermediate forms agree with this plan, but *Leptoceratops,* from the uppermost Cretaceous of North America, appears to be the exception. (Particularly as it lived at the same time as the large *Pentaceratops* and *Arrhinoceratops;* the remains of all three having been found in the Edmonton beds of Alberta.)

Leptoceratops attained a length of only 2 metres (6·5 feet), approximately one fifth that of its great cousins. The head was characteristically deep with a narrow snout, but the bird-like beak was less pronounced. At the back of the skull the frill took the form of a solid shield which covered the neck, but not the shoulders. The body, like the head, shows considerable differences when compared with those of its contemporaries; the fore limbs being considerably shorter than the back ones. *Leptoceratops* was lightly built, and the suggestion is that it spent part of its life in a bipedal pose. The frill offered none of the protection of those of the larger species, and it is probable that *Leptoceratops* spent much of its life in forest areas, grazing on the lower levels of vegetation.

In times of danger, *Leptoceratops* would run rather than face an enemy. The fact that *Leptoceratops* existed alongside more advanced individuals presents a palaeontological problem, which could have two answers. As the first, one could suggest that *Leptoceratops* had existed undiscovered for several million years, and that it was ideally suited to its environment. Structurally it would have remained unchanged throughout time, whilst descendants developed into more and more bizarre creatures. The alternative answer is that *Leptoceratops* itself represented an unusual development, evolving at a late stage in the history of the ceratopsians to occupy a previously abandoned niche. The evidence in support of either of these is debatable, and one would only suggest from the preserved material that *Leptoceratops* was a successful member of the Upper Cretaceous Ceratopsia. In life, the small horned dinosaur would probably have shared its environment with the herds of hadrosaurs that flourished throughout the western region of North America.

Styracosaurus

(Greek, spiky lizard)

Styracosaurus was a short-frilled ceratopsian which existed during the Upper Cretaceous, over 65 million years ago. It was a herbivore which lived in herds on the open lands of North America. The body was bulky, like those of related genera, and the tail was relatively short and thick. It was typically quadrupedal, the feet being broad and short with the toes ending in small, hoof-like structures. The animal grazed, with the use of its beak and strong cheek teeth, on low, shrub-like vegetation. Behind the beak the skull bore a large nasal horn similar to that of the present day rhinoceros. Two smaller horns occurred behind the eyes. *Styracosaurus* had a moderately large frill over the neck, the back edge of which was formed into a number of large and spectacular spikes. The function of the frill was obviously one of protection, and the spikes not only added to this but also gave the animal a rather fearsome profile. Face on, *Styracosaurus* would have looked quite spectacular, with a nasal horn of over half a metre (1·6 feet) placed in the centre of a 1·2 metre (4 foot) wide frill.

Styracosaurus shared its Upper Cretaceous environment with several other types of horned dinosaurs and numerous species of crested hadrosaurs. Both lowland and upland areas supported herbivorous populations, and these in turn supported meat-eating and egg-stealing stocks. The egg stealer was *Ornithomimus*, and *Gorgosaurus* was the incumbent carnosaur. It is unlikely that the meat eater deliberately set out to feed on *Styracosaurus*, especially as easier prey was to be found close by. On the rare occasions when the two confronted each other, the horned dinosaur would turn and charge its foe at considerable speed. Recent estimates of the speeds achieved by these creatures have reached as high as 48 kilometres per hour (30 miles per hour). These estimates were based on the study of the limb joints, and are related to the theory that the dinosaurs were warm-blooded. If these figures are true, the clash of these formidable creatures would have been a truly spectacular sight. Certain scientific texts have recorded the presence of *Styracosaurus* in the Upper Cretaceous deposits of Mongolia. If these are correct then the distribution of the 'spiny ceratopsian' would be further support for the idea of a land link between North America and Asia some 70 million years ago. The link is thought to have existed across the Bering Straits.

Monoclonius

(Greek, single horn)

Geological formations such as the Lance, Hell Creek, Edmonton and Belly River series, have yielded a great deal of material and information important to the reconstruction of the ceratopsian family tree. These deposits occur in western North America and represent approximately 30 million years of geological time. They are comparable in age with similar deposits in Mongolia and China, from which horned dinosaurs have also been collected. The origins of the horned dinosaurs probably rest in Asia, but by the Upper Cretaceous the group had crossed on to the North American land mass. Sediments of the Belly River series are the oldest of the above sequence, and it follows that the ceratopsian remains they contain represent an early phase in the evolution of the group.

The remains indicate that the individual forms had increased considerably in size and that two distinct lines had emerged. *Monoclonius* and *Styracosaurus* represented the so-called short-frilled ceratopsians, whilst *Chasmosaurus* was a long-frilled type. To many palaeontologists *Monoclonius* represents the direct link between the ancestral form *Protoceratops* and the great *Triceratops*. The first remains of *Monoclonius* were found in 1914, the complete skeleton measuring just under 6 metres (19·5 feet) in length, which represents a three-fold increase over that of its ancestor. Although classified as a short-frilled ceratopsian, *Monoclonius* measured 2 metres (6·5 feet) from the tip of the snout to the back edge of the frill. In most respects *Monoclonius* was typical, being a large, quadrupedal herbivore with a relatively short but bulky tail. Facially, however, it was different for it had a long, single horn rising from the top of the nose. Small brow horns occurred one over each eye, but they were relatively insignificant.

During the early part of the Upper Cretaceous *Monoclonius* roamed the lands of North America in large herds. They searched for succulent vegetation which grew on the edges of the great forests and were quiet, inoffensive creatures. It was likely that they could run quite quickly and would group together in times of danger. In full flight *Monoclonius* would have looked very similar to a modern rhinoceros, although its size and great head shield would make it an even more formidable adversary. Even a great carnosaur would have thought twice before attacking the 'single horn', for one false move would have resulted in death.

Brachylophosaurus

(Greek, short-crested lizard)

Brachylophosaurus is one of the best known of the flat-headed hadrosaurs, or duck-billed dinosaurs. It lived in the Upper Cretaceous forests of North America, where it browsed on the leaves and twigs of flowering plants. As a flat-headed hadrosaur, *Brachylophosaurus* lacked the bony growths of many of its contemporaries. It stood about 5 metres (16·5 feet) tall, and the face was rather deep and narrow, although the nasal bones did form a broad, flat shield over the front of the skull. In the great crested hadrosaurs such as *Corythosaurus* or *Parasaurolophus*, the crests are seen as indicators of rank within a herd. The largest males had the largest crests, and a display of anger would have been enough to drive off the challenge of a younger animal. In *Brachylophosaurus* the absence of the crest places the importance on to the bony shield. It was flat and broad, as described above, and its position on the snout suggests that it was a defence or combative mechanism. In defence the plate would be used to absorb or deflect a blow from an opponent or rival. Opponents could include the horned dinosaurs, whilst a rival would come from inside its own herd. In a battle for the leadership of the herd and selection of the strongest females, the male brachylophosaurs would enter into a competition of head pushing. Similar rituals are to be seen among modern-day deer with the strongest males dominating the herd. In many ways this combat ensures the survival of the fittest and the development of a healthy family stock. Further evidence of this function for the plate is seen in the protection of the eyes and nostrils by a thickening of the overlying bones. Intra-herd combats would hardly ever have resulted in bodily harm to either of the participants.

Similar struggles for dominance may have taken place in the more 'duck-billed' types but in these cases the flat beaks were used to do the pushing. Against an enemy such as *Gorgosaurus*, *Brachylophosaurus* was defenceless and one can only suggest that in times of danger the herd fled to safety. As *Brachylophosaurus* lacks the crests and frills of other hadrosaurs, it would appear to represent a rather primitive but quite persistent condition within the evolution of the group. *Brachylophosaurus* was very similar to its ancestor *Kritosaurus*, which possessed a similar, but smaller, shield over the snout.

Pachycephalosaurus

(Greek, thick-headed lizard)

The dome-headed dinosaurs were one of the most curious groups of ornithopods to appear during the Upper Cretaceous. In many ways they were similar to forms such as the iguanodonts or hypsilophodontids, but the development of their heads was unique. In *Pachycephalosaurus* the jaws were in some ways primitive with a rather weak dentition, but above the jaws and behind the eyes, the skull was expanded into a grotesque dome. Spikes and small bony swellings formed a half ring or 'ornamental' area at the back of the skull. The dome of *Pachycephalosaurus* was over 22 centimetres (8·5 inches) thick, and one would suggest that this was rather excessive if intended solely for the protection of a very small brain.

Like other ornithopods *Pachycephalosaurus* was a herding animal which lived in the open lands of North America, Europe and Asia. Its herd structure was carefully organized, with groups of females and young animals dominated by the largest males. As with modern deer or mountain goats, the males would have had to protect their territory against younger intruders, who on maturity would seek to establish their own group. In order to drive off the young pretender, the leader would enter into a trial of strength, both individuals using their heads as battering rams. The pachycephalosaurs were bipedal, and it is probable that the males ran towards each other at considerable speed. The males would battle until one or the other emerged in triumph, to roam his territory with head held high in a show of visual dominance. Within the herd the size of the dome was an important indication of the rank of an individual animal. The threat of an attack from a carnosaur was always a possibility during the Upper Cretaceous, and it is likely that, once cornered, the male pachycephalosaurs could have turned and butted their tormentor whilst the herd escaped. Usually, however, these rather small ornithopods would have turned and fled. In some environmental reconstructions the pachycephalosaurs are seen as mountain or hill-dwelling creatures, their size and comparative agility enabling them to exist in areas where no carnosaur would roam. This interpretation would draw them even closer to the niche now occupied by the mountain sheep or goats. Unlike these animals, however, the pachycephalosaurs, as stated previously, had a weak dentition and would have found coarse upland vegetation difficult to consume.

Parasaurolophus

(Greek, abnormal crested lizard)

The success of the duck-billed dinosaurs, or hadrosaurs, during the Upper Cretaceous is reflected in the variety of species found throughout the Northern Hemisphere. The body was similar in form throughout the whole family, but the heads varied enormously. *Parasaurolophus* was among the most spectacular of the crested hadrosaurs, the hollow crest extending well beyond the back of the skull. The length of the backward projection varied between species and possibly within families, where large males would have had the longest crests. The most spectacular crests were to be found in the form *Parasaurolophus tubicens* in which structures of over 1·5 metres (5 feet) have been recorded. As it is hollow, the crest was once considered to have acted as a chamber for the storage of air, which was used when the animal swam under water. This inferred that *Parasaurolophus* either lived in water or sought refuge there in times of trouble. Unfortunately the capacity of the chamber was extremely limited and the amount of air it contained would have been of little use to such a large creature. A fully aquatic mode of life was also unlikely for an animal which possessed batteries of crushing teeth and hoofed feet. The crushing teeth and the contents of a mummified stomach indicate that the hadrosaurs fed on quite tough plant material; whilst the short, hoofed feet suggest movement over a firm terrain.

Parasaurolophus browsed on pine, oak and poplar on the outer edges of the Upper Cretaceous forests. It lived in herds and, like its modern day counterparts, the herbivorous mammals, was ever alert to danger. Sight, sound and smell were important and it is possible that the tubular interior of the crest was covered with sensitive tissue, which improved the sense of smell. *Parasaurolophus* may have also developed a 'voice' – or rather a bellow – like that of the crocodiles, which would have been used to warn the herd of impending danger or to frighten off unwanted males during the breeding season. The form of the crest and related frill were also important in the recognition of territorial boundaries and as sex display features. In the regions where *Parasaurolophus* lived, numerous other hadrosaurs existed at the same time, and the identification of their own kind would have proved difficult if, like the body, the heads were less distinctive. It is extremely unlikely that *Parasaurolophus* used the hollow crest as an offensive weapon; in times of danger it would have turned and ran.

Corythosaurus

(Greek, helmet lizard)

Corythosaurus was one of a large number of different duck-billed dinosaurs that lived during the Upper Cretaceous. It was a crested duck bill in which the crest, unlike that of *Brachylophosaurus*, was hollow. *Corythosaurus* was a typically large ornithopod which grew to over 9 metres (29·5 feet) in length. The body conformed to the normal hadrosaur pattern, but the head and crest exhibited a number of diagnostic characters. Facially the beak was very narrow and less duck-like than in *Anatosaurus*. The crest was large and helmet-like, being formed by an expansion of certain bones at the front of the skull. Internally, a pair of elongate nasal passages extended into the crest, where they linked up with a larger looped chamber.

The function of these complex structures has been the subject of much debate, and each theory suggests a different mode of life for the animal. One suggestion is that the crest functioned as a snorkel device to help the animal either feed under water or hide there from an attacker. Unfortunately the pressure of water outside the head would be greater than that within, and the animal would have drowned. A second theory relates the increase in size of the passageways with an improvement in the sense of smell. This last theory is strongly supported, for it would indicate the development of an advance warning system in an otherwise unprotected dinosaur. A third theory related to *Corythosaurus* is that the crests represent adaptations to social functions within a herd. In this case the crests would vary with size and sex and would be related to identification, signalling and combat. A recent review of the various forms referred to *Corythosaurus* suggests that this third theory may be correct and that instead of six species, we have only the males, females and juveniles of a single stock.

Crest variety in *Corythosaurus* was important to the successful mating of similar individuals, and the continuation of the family line. In life the corythosaurs moved in herds with the males made recognizable by the larger dimensions of their crests. The crests acted as indicators of rank, with young males and females possessing smaller structures. As herbivores, these hadrosaurs were almost defenceless and it is not suprising therefore to learn that they had developed a keen sense of hearing. The approach of a carnosaur would be soon detected and the herd would flee to safer grounds.

Scolosaurus

(Greek, crooked lizard)

The evolution of the armoured dinosaurs, the ankylosaurs, reached its climax during the Upper Cretaceous. Numerous genera existed in many parts of the world, with the majority of the different types occurring on the North American land mass. *Scolosaurus* lived in the western region of this area and shared its environment with numerous other herbivores and the ever-present carnivores. Although closely related to earlier forms such as *Acanthopholis* from the Cretaceous of Europe, *Scolosaurus* was much more heavily armoured. In fact the two genera are examples of the two families that exist within the Ankylosauria, the less heavily armoured forms representing the more primitive stock.

Scolosaurus was an advanced ankylosaur (or nodosaur), and its armour took the form of a pavement of bony plates which covered the upper part of the body from nose to tail. Over the shoulders and the trunk region the plates adopted a transverse pattern, with low, vertical spines giving the animal a rather spiky appearance. The head was carried low and the eyes were rather small and well protected. Like all ankylosaurs, *Scolosaurus* was quadrupedal, having a sprawling gait similar to that of earlier, more primitive reptiles. In the case of *Scolosaurus*, however, this stance was somewhat protective, the whole body being placed quite close to the ground with a low centre of gravity. In times of danger *Scolosaurus* simply adopted a squat position, its body armour and 3·5 tonnes of weight enabling it to resist the challenge of most carnivores. The tail of *Scolosaurus* ended in a large club-like structure armed with two sharp, vertical spines. It is unlikely that this structure was purely ornamental, and it suggests that the animal might even have taken the initiative against an enemy. The body armour of *Scolosaurus* was flexible, and it is likely that under attack the animal drew the head close to the body. As with other ankylosaurs, *Scolosaurus* had small, bead-like teeth which suggests that the animal fed on soft vegetation.

Because of its squat appearance and weight, it is more than likely that *Scolosaurus* lived above the swamplands, in areas of abundant plant growth and firm terrain. Although the actual number of ankylosaurs found as fossils is small, the variety of individual types, together with the survival of the group throughout the Cretaceous Period, indicate that they adapted very successfully to a plant-eating way of life.

Euoplocephalus

(Greek, well-protected head)

Throughout the descriptive history of the dinosaurs, the skeletons of a given animal have in some cases been given a different name by different authors. This may arise out of error, or because the scientists concerned both believe they have a unique specimen. In time, the specimens will be compared, and the earliest or senior name will be selected to represent the group or individual. This problem arose between the specimens named *Euoplocephalus* and *Ankylosaurus* and, as the former was the older name, it received priority. In some ways this is unfortunate for the group, the ankylosaurs, received their name from the type genus *Ankylosaurus*.

Euoplocephalus and its close relatives succeeded the stegosaurs of the early Cretaceous. The ankylosaurs of the Upper Cretaceous were heavily armoured and are often described as reptilian 'tanks'. In *Euoplocephalus* the body was flattened and covered by an armour of thick, bony plates. In fact the cover was so complete that it extended from the snout to the club-like structure at the end of the tail. The head was relatively small and the jaws were bordered by rows of very small teeth. *Euoplocephalus* was quadrupedal, the fore limbs being shorter than the hind limbs. The body was held quite close to the ground and the rise of the back towards the pelvis was less noticeable than in the stegosaurs. Its feet were short and broad, possibly padded underneath to absorb some of the shock when its weight of 5 tonnes pressed against the earth. The animal was slow when compared with the bipedal carnosaurs, and the armour was essential for defence. Unable to outrun its predator, the ankylosaur would squat low on the ground, the body protected against slashing blows from the carnosaur's feet. An adult *Euoplocephalus*, 5 metres (16·5 feet) in length, would be relatively safe, as the carnosaur would be unable to turn it over and attack the softer belly region. A juvenile would be less fortunate, however, and a persistent predator would ultimately succeed in turning and killing its prey. It is possible that the tail of *Euoplocephalus*, with its club-like end, was used in battle. It could have deterred a carnosaur by adding to its frustration, for a blow landed with accuracy would have inflicted considerable pain. The tail may also have been used in territorial battles, when the males of the ankylosaur herds chose their mates and defended their breeding grounds.

Anatosaurus

(Greek, duck reptile)

During the Upper Cretaceous the hadrosaurian dinosaurs became one of the most successful groups of herbivores. They were bipedal ornithischians whose remains have been found throughout the Northern Hemisphere. Numerous genera have been described, with the ancestry of the group being traced back to a hypothetical iguanodont. The hadrosaurian family tree culminated in the appearance of *Anatosaurus* during the uppermost part of the Cretaceous Period. In the past, the remains of *Anatosaurus* were referred to several species, but in 1970 and again in 1975 it was proposed that they belonged to the one species *Anatosaurus annectens*.

Like other hadrosaurs, *Anatosaurus* was characterized by massive, strong back legs. The feet were large, with the three toes terminating in blunt, hoof-like structures. These were hardly the appropriate appendages for the swamp-dwelling or semi-aquatic mode of life often suggested for the animal. *Anatosaurus* grew to over 10 metres (33 feet) in length and weighed several tonnes; from the evidence of pine needles, twigs, fruits and seeds found in the stomach of a mummified animal, *Anatosaurus* appears to have been a terrestrial herbivore. Recent reconstructions of the animal suggest that it could run very quickly, with the tail held in the horizontal position. Vast herds of these hadrosaurs thrived during the Upper Cretaceous, roaming through forests in search of food. The body of *Anatosaurus* was similar to that of earlier genera but its head was quite different. Unlike the lambeosaurines or saurolophines it lacked a crest and possessed no nasal hump like the early kritosaurs. Instead the anterior area of the skull was expanded to form the familiar duck-bill structure; with the nostrils positioned high on the face. This development was without doubt related to its feeding habits, but would also serve a second function as a sex display character.

The different species of past 'authors' may therefore represent the variety of individuals within a herd. Large males would have been recognizable by having the broadest bill, whilst females and juveniles would be identified by smaller structures. Apart from the stomach contents, mummified remains have also provided information on the skin of *Anatosaurus*. Texturally this was similar to that of a modern day crocodile, with minute tubercles in place of large bony ossicles or scutes. Evidence also exists to show that *Anatosaurus* had a small frill along its back and a web-like arrangement between the fingers of the hand.

Triceratops

(Greek, three-horned face)

Triceratops, like *Iguanodon, Tyrannosaurus* and *Stegosaurus,* is one of the best-known dinosaurs although, when its horns were first discovered in 1877, they were attributed to the mammal *Bison alticornis. Triceratops* was a horned dinosaur which roamed in herds over the open lands of North America during the uppermost Cretaceous. The herds included animals of all sizes, ranging from juveniles to giant males, many of which reached over 7 metres (23 feet) in length and weighed 7 or 8 tonnes. Several species of *Triceratops* are known from Alberta (Canada), Montana and Wyoming (United States), and it is likely that individual herds represented a single species. The overall form of the various species was very similar, but the length of the horns, the position of the eyes and the shape of the frill were sufficiently different to warrant the allocation of separate names.

In general *Triceratops* was a heavily built, quadrupedal ornithischian. The head was massive; an animal of 6 to 8 metres (19·5 to 26 feet) in length having a skull of over 2 metres (6·5 feet). Features of the skull included the parrot-like beak, three horns and the large frill which extended backwards over the neck. The beak was used to pull and clip vegetation, which was then cut and chewed between the teeth of the upper and lower jaws. The nose horn of *Triceratops* was quite small but the brow horns reached enormous proportions, with some reaching nearly 1 metre (3 feet) in length. Behind the horns, the broad frill gave ample protection to the neck area.

Travelling in herds the great ceratopsians would be fairly safe; their large numbers offering them considerable protection against a marauding carnosaur. Isolated, however, individuals would be attacked and the great horns would be used as weapons on which an unwary carnosaur could find itself impaled. *Triceratops* was in many ways the reptilian 'rhinoceros' of the late Cretaceous and, like its modern day mammalian equivalent, it would have been a difficult creature to corner and kill. It was one of the last of the numerous horned dinosaurs of North America and Asia; its success was related to its ability to meet change and fill the niches vacated by earlier forms. In the Late Cretaceous, the changing climate and vegetation were responsible for the demise of many herbivorous dinosaurs, and *Triceratops*, without competition, was able to increase in numbers.

Tyrannosaurus

(Greek, tyrant lizard)

Of all the dinosaurs, *Tyrannosaurus rex* the 'king of the tyrant lizards' is probably the best known. It lived in the Upper Cretaceous environments of North America and Mongolia, some 75–70 million years ago. *Tyrannosaurus* was an enormous creature over 5 metres (16 feet) tall and 8 tonnes in weight. From its nose to the tip of its tail the giant carnosaur measured approximately 13 metres (42 feet). Its head was enormous, the jaws were over 1 metre (3 feet) in length and were armed with numerous 15 cm (6 inch) teeth. Apart from their size, the teeth were serrated and must have been very efficient weapons. The jaw mechanism allowed the mouth to open extremely wide, and *Tyrannosaurus* was capable of tearing off and swallowing enormous pieces of its victim's flesh. In contrast to the enormous size of the head, the fore limbs were minute structures which, apart from helping the animal to rise from a resting position, were almost useless. The hands had but two clawed fingers and were extremely limited structures.

No-one doubts that *Tyrannosaurus* was a bipedal predator, although the way in which it ran has been the subject of some considerable discussion Early palaeontologists thought that the beast moved along with an almost upright stance, dragging its tail behind it. Recently these views have been questioned, and *Tyrannosaurus* is now thought to have run rather quickly, its body held in an almost horizontal position. As with other carnosaurs, the 'tyrant lizard' moved with a distinct waddle, successive footprints appearing one behind the other. The enormous hind feet were bird-like, three of the four toes having extremely large claws. A blow from the hind leg would have severely injured any contemporary animal.

Tyrannosaurus preyed on the herds of dinosaurs that roamed the Upper Cretaceous plains. A likely victim was the horned *Triceratops,* large numbers of which occurred at the same time as *Tyrannosaurus.* In recent scientific publications this well-armoured ceratopsian has been compared with the rhinoceros, and attributed with a top speed of 48 kilometres per hour (30 miles per hour). To capture and kill such fast-moving prey, *Tyrannosaurus* itself must have been an astounding creature and would fully warrant its somewhat emotive name. Other victims of *Tyrannosaurus* included the large, bipedal hadrosaurs, many of which flourished in the environments of the uppermost Cretaceous. To suggest that *Tyrannosaurus* was an extremely active creature would infer that it needed a constant supply of food to sustain its energy level. To hunt continuously was impossible even for *Tyrannosaurus,* and it is probable that like other large dinosaurs it was extremely efficient in conserving its energy.

Index

Page numbers in italics refer to illustrations

Books to read

Charig, A. and Horsfield, B. 1975 *Before the Ark*. B.B.C. publications, London.

Colbert, E. H. 1962 *Dinosaurs – their discovery and their world*. Hutchinson, London.

Cox, C. B. 1976 *Prehistoric Animals*. Hamlyn, London.

Halstead, L. B. 1975 *The evolution and ecology of the Dinosaurs*. Peter Lowe, London.

Moody, R. 1976 *The World of Dinosaurs*. Hamlyn, London.

Romer, A. S. 1967 *Vertebrate Palaeontology*. University of Chicago Press.